Welcome to the world of

WINE

This is a fascinating time for wine, not least because it's getting more and more difficult to draw a line between Old and New Worlds. Even in New Zealand, credited with kick-starting the New Wave movement with its extraordinary pea-pod and kiwi-fruit sauvignons, some Old World ideas are gaining ground. In France, Italy, and Spain—heartlands of the Old World wine culture—New Wave ideas and methods are steadily creeping in. So far this is very good news, particularly for inexpensive wine, which thanks to improved fruit and cleaner wine conditions, has made a spectacular leap forward in quality.

There has never been a better time to set out to explore the world of wine.

No passport required.

D0557340

Other HarperEssentials

FIRST AID
STRESS SURVIVAL GUIDE
UNDERSTANDING DREAMS

HARPERESSENTIALS

Wine Guide

Andrea Gillies

HarperTorch
An Imprint of HarperCollinsPublishers

This book was originally published by HarperCollins UK in 1999.

❤ HARPERTORCH
An Imprint of HarperCollins*Publishers*
10 East 53rd Street
New York, New York 10022-5299

First HarperTorch paperback printing: August 2003

CONTENTS

Introduction

Welcome to the new edition of *HarperEssentials Wine Guide*. As ever, the guide brings all the important trends, news and tips from the world of wine, as well as hundreds of suggestions of wines to look out for in stores, all packaged up in a very handy pocket-sized volume.

Using the guide

The guide is arranged in order of country, starting with Argentina and ending in the USA. Fizz, the last chapter, also includes champagne. The country chapters are laid out straightforwardly. Most follow the New World model and are organized under grape, whites first, reds second: thus Chardonnay, Riesling and Sauvignon Blanc are followed by Cabernet Sauvignon, Merlot and Shiraz. In France and Italy, where appellations still rule, wines are arranged under AC and DOC order, though grape variety classifications are creeping in even here. Where appropriate, individual wines are suggested. These are listed in ascending order of price, cheapest first, most expensive last:

Y = under $8
YY = under $15
YYY = between $15 and $30
($12.00) in some cases a figure in brackets follow-
            ing the wine name gives a specific price

These were the prices at the time of going to press. Be aware that price tags change, usually for the worse. The vast majority of wines mentioned are available on the high street, in supermarkets, off-licenses and wine merchants. If you can't find the particular brand listed, try something from the same producer, region or appellation, and please do write in with any startling discoveries.

Old World, New World

There are a few terms bandied about in wine-speak that may require a little definition. Old World and New World are key phrases. Old World is basically Europe, as you might expect, but not only geographically. (Ironically, some of the most entrenched Old World wine-making is to be found in the so-called New World, in the country wineries of Argentina.) Old World wine-making is all about traditional, centuries-old methods. Grapes are now seldom crushed by human feet, but the old ways of growing, harvesting, fermenting and aging wine, often involving extensive use of wooden barrels, are still very much with us. This is sometimes a good thing. But not always. New World wine-making is a concept that's only been with us on a commercial scale for 20 years but is already the norm in many countries, notably Australia, New Zealand, Chile, South Africa and California. At its most extreme, the New World ethos treats the vineyards as a giant laboratory. Fruit is grown, picked and handled in the most scientific way possible, fermented in cool conditions, the wine made in stainless steel. It may or may not see some wood fermentation or aging—if so this is very likely to be in new (very new) French or American oak, and in a highly controlled, contrived manner. The objective is the cleanest, purest, most fruit-driven style of wine obtainable. New World (also called New Wave) wine-making has introduced the varietal—wines named by their grape variety—to a world where previously this idea was pretty much confined to Alsace. Now wines calling themselves Chardonnay and Pinot Noir are commonplace, even in the Côte d'Or region of France, where previously only white and red Burgundy were referred to.

This is a fascinating time for wine, not least because it's getting more and more difficult to draw a line between Old and New Worlds. Even in New Zealand, credited with kick-starting the New Wave movement with its extraordinary, pea-pod and kiwi-fruit Sauvignons, some Old World ideas are creeping in. (A short aside here. Apparently the stainless steel fermenting tank that now symbolizes the New Wave all over the globe was an innocent by-product of all that shiny equipment used in New Zealand dairy farming. New Zealand wine-growers thought they'd have a go, using tanks surplus to requirements in the milk industry. The rest, as they say, is history.) In France, Italy and Spain, heartlands of the Old World wine culture, New Wave ideas and methods are steadily creeping in. So far this is very good news, particularly for cheap wine, which thanks to improved fruit and cleaner winery conditions has made a spectacular leap forward in quality. At the other side of the world, in Australia, producers are beginning to tire of their consistent, fruity, squeaky clean, international style reds and whites, and are looking to European traditions for ways of making something more individual, more local, that tastes of its place, its sun and soil. Many of the best and most creative winemakers have found it is possible to marry the Old and New Worlds, and are making fantastic wines that have rich pure fruit, but also personality and shape and layers of flavor.

We are going through a period of huge change, as the New World wine regions grow up and mature. Though internationalism can go too far: there is now a nominally South African wine which blends wines from three continents—Chilean Sauvignon Blanc, Australian Chardonnay, and home-grown Colombard-Chardonnay, chucking in bags of oak chips for that "oak-aged sophistication." But there are more optimistic trends. The phenomenal success of the New World wine industry has provided the cash and experience to make changes for the better. All over the world growers are grubbing up unsuccessful grape varieties and replanting. This could be a worrying trend—after all, does the world really need more Chardonnay and Cabernet Sauvignon? But in general it's a good thing if it means farewell to masses of useless Chenin Blanc in South Africa, and to mediocre German varieties in England (er, and in Germany too); to the introduction and success of obscure French grapes in Australia, and obscure Italians in Argentina.

There has never been a better time to set out to explore the world of wine. No passport required.

Andrea Gillies

ARGENTINA

Some wine critics say that it's full steam ahead for Argentina now, and watch out world, following the phenomenally good 1999 vintage. Others warn that Argentina is faltering, stuck in a formulaic rut (Chile and South Africa also get this criticism). What's clear is that Argentina has embarked on a season of change, and while whites are perhaps a bit rustic, reds are improving in leaps and bounds, particularly with European varietals like Tempranillo (Spain), Sangiovese (Italy) and Syrah (France). There is, it's true, a lot of cheap dull wine. But there is also lots of cheap exciting wine of a quality hard to find elsewhere—this is still a good country for wine under $8. More excitingly, there is more and more world class red. It's slower to come than predicted, but it's still coming.

There's still a strong feeling that Argentina is a sleeping giant. A few producers with imagination are creating the reputation, but there are also 2000 wineries out there plodding along like they always have, making rustic wine for the home market. In Argentina it's still important to look to the producer rather than the grape variety or region. La Agricola (Familia Zuccardi Q, Santa Julia, Picajuan Peak), Balbi, Bianchi, Catena, Esmeralda (Alamos, Catena, Argento), Etchart, Fabre Montmayou, Lurton, Norton, Trapiche and Weinert are some of the names to keep an eye out for.

Mendoza, the engine room of the Argentinian wine industry, produces 80% of Argentinian wine. It's 1000 miles inland from the Atlantic, protected from the Pacific by the Andes, and only 100 miles east of Santiago, Chile's capital, though mountains over 20,000 feet high separate the two countries. Most vineyards are planted on scrubby rocky soil; there's good drainage, but low rainfall, so irrigation is the key. Some old Inca irrigation systems are still in use. The looming presence of mountains also means that cool microclimates can be used for whites and for cool-climate loving reds, so Argentina has immense vinous versatility. This is, incredibly, the fifth largest wine producer in the world by volume, though the wine industry here is really only five years old as a quality industry, since the rapturous reception given to the 1996 vintage. The home market still tends to prefer its wine oaky and "winey" in an old-fashioned sense, rather than fruity, so producers tend to make wine in two styles, one for home and another, more fruit-driven, for export. The quality of fruit is breathtakingly good and growing conditions, in a good year, so perfect that, as in Chile, grape varieties can have an astonishing intensity

Another reason Argentinian wine has such fruity purity is the good clean air and water of the Andean foothills—very little herbicide is used here, and indeed La Agricola is in the process of going totally organic. Agricola's vineyards are extraordinary—not only do they use the old-fashioned canopy system in which fruit hangs down freely from its roof of leaves, but they have state-of-the-art anti-hail nets (hail is a big problem in Mendoza) and anti-frost lamps. If the temperature falls below a certain level members of an anti-frost hit squad are called from their beds to come and ward off the cold.

Waves of immigration have made the Argentinian wine culture the way it is—the French brought Merlot, Cabernet and Malbec, the Italians Barbera and Sangiovese (via 18th century monks), the Spanish Torrontés and Tempranillo. Now foreign input is important again as a huge influx of investment and expertise takes hold. It's beginning to pay off. 1999 was a great year and the way ahead looks very rosy.

VINTAGES

1998 was troubled, because of El Niño reeking its customary havoc, but '99 was excellent. 2000 was again troubled by harsh weather at harvest. Quantity will be down but quality good at the better end. Look out for '99s lingering on shelves. 1995/6/7 were excellent vintages.

GRAPE VARIETIES

WHITES

Chardonnay World class Chardonnay was expected but Argentina hasn't delivered yet, though there are noble exceptions. There has been a tapering-off at the top end, though the mid-range is stuffed with goodies. Argento Chardonnay is amazing value at just $8. Creamy, oaked Chardonnays are the coming thing, with rich, buttery, nutty flavors. More tropical notes are beginning to appear—the trick is to keep these blowsy, ripe exotic characteristics in check.

🍷 Lost Pampas Oaked Chardonnay • Argento Chardonnay • Bright Brothers San Juan Chardonnay • Martins Chardonnay

🍷🍷 Viña Amalia Chardonnay • Alamos Chardonnay • Santa Julia Reserve Chardonnay • Catena Chardonnay, Agrelo vineyards

Chardonnay Blends There's great potential here but very little coming through as yet. Semillon is a big hit in Australia so ought to translate well to Argentinian conditions.

🍷 Norton Semillon Chardonnay

Chenin Blanc Argentina hasn't really got to grips with Chenin yet. Retailers have cut their Chenin wines as a result. Whether Argentina will persist with Chenin experiments remains to be seen. Previous attempts have been thin and too cheap, rather like the dire Chenin lake of the Cape. Bad ones are lean and thin, or pointlessly fat and very dull to drink. Good ones are both crisp and rich, perhaps with delicate pear fruit and a hint of lanolin.

Pinot Gris Most Argentinian Pinot Gris underwhelm, but the good ones have apricot subtlety and a delicate fresh dryness.
🍷 Bodega Lurton Pinot Gris • Corazon Pinot Gris

Torrontés It was said that Tor-rontés had the potential to become another Chardonnay but only a few producers seem to be able to make it work. This is surprising because at its best Torrontés is a deliciously creamy, nutty, spicy white. Unfortunately most is over-cropped, high yields leading to dilute flavors. Badly made examples abound, many with a curiously synthetic, perfumy note.
🍷 Norton Torrontés

Bodega
NORTON

Since 1895

2000
TORRONTES
MENDOZA
Vino Fino Blanco
Envasado en origen Bodega Norton S.A.
Luján de Cuyo, Mendoza
12% vol   ARGENTINA   75 cl.e

Viognier Up and coming, as is its sister Rhône variety, the Syrah. Good ones have delicate peach character, both rich and dry. Santa Julia's is made in a bolder style, an impressive wine for a mere $8.

🍷 Far Flung Viognier • Santa Julia Viognier
🍷🍷 Santa Julia Voignier Reserve

REDS

Barbera Experiments with Barbera have had mixed success, but the occasional high class beauty like Balbi's has masses of fruit, depth and personality. Rich dark autumnal notes make it a good food red.

🍷🍷🍷 Balbi Barbera

Bonarda Bonarda is everywhere now, a fashionable variety. It can still tend to the ripe and soupy, lacking balancing acids and tannins, but good Bonardas have a juicy, savory-sweet quaffability, making them good with herby food and ethnic dishes.

🍷 Adiseno Bonarda • Picajuan Peak Bonarda • Corazon Bonarda
🍷🍷 Alamos Bonarda

Cabernet Franc Long used in Argentinian style "clarets" but fairly new as a single varietal. More will follow.

🍷🍷 Bin 99 Argentine Cabernet Franc

Cabernet Sauvignon Argentinian Cabernet can be a

revelation—Zuccardi and Bianchi make top class
wines fit to cause
receiving hairlines
in Bordeaux; these
wines will age and
improve in bottle.
There's still plenty
of good $8–$9 wine
about too. Cassis-

drenched, intense, with plum and strawberry fruit,
tobacco and chocolate, lush warm tannins and a firm
structure, good Argentinian Cabernet is of world class.
Two years ago the cheapies were hard and leafy—now
thanks to improved techniques they tend to be merely
fruity and anonymously international in style.

🍷 Bright Bros. San Juan Cabernet Sauvignon

🍷🍷 Norton Cabernet Sauvignon • Alamos Cabernet
Sauvignon • Trapiche Oak Reserve Cabernet Sauvignon •
Viña Amalia Cabernet Sauvignon • Valentin Bianchi
Cabernet Sauvignon • Catena Cabernet Sauvignon

🍷🍷🍷 Carmello Patti Cabernet Sauvignon •
Q Cabernet Sauvignon, Zuccardi • Famiglia Bianchi
Cabernet Sauvignon

Malbec No one does Malbec like Argentina.
A world away from the black wines of Cahors
in south west France and from its lowly supporting role in the great blends of Bordeaux,
Argentinian Malbec is unlike any other wine.
A great brooding monster of fruit and spice
and leather and savory, rubbery notes in its

concentrated, boutique winery manifestations. It can also be damson-rich, dry yet sweet, creamily tannic even at the cheap end of the spectrum, though some modern mid-price wines are merely juicy, which is to miss the point of the Malbec character. The key note is a lingering savory quality. Some are very rich, some earthy, with a delicately charred flavor. . . . Creosote? Is anyone else getting creosote?

> "a great brooding monster of fruit and spice and leather and savory, rubbery notes"

🍷 Argento Malbec • Valentin Bianchi Malbec
🍷🍷 Anubis Malbec • Diego Murillo Family Reserve Malbec, Patagonia • Fabre Montmayou Malbec • Santa Julia Malbec Oak Reserve • Viña Amalia Malbec • Ricardo Santos Malbec • Weinert Malbec

Merlot After a disappointing phase, Merlot vineyard sites are now being worked on and rejigged, so expect steep improvements in Merlot quality to follow. Meanwhile you need to pay top dollar for the good stuff— there's a big divide between the rich, leathery, elegant Merlot of Valentin Bianchi's Reserve and simple plummy quaffers at the $8 level, which are merely soft and ripe.

🍷🍷 Norton Merlot • Alamos Merlot • Fabre Montmayou Merlot • Q Merlot, Zuccardi
🍷🍷🍷 Valentin Bianchi Merlot Reserve

Sangiovese Italianate reds, soft and ripe at the budget

end, richer and herby at the boutique winery end. Few come up with a recognizably tea-baggy, orange zesty character of the Chianti original. Doing well in blends, with Bonarda or even Malbec. Lots of potential, lots more good wine in the pipeline.

♟ Picajuan Peak Sangiovese

Shiraz Previously confined to Australian style, irreverently Rhône-Bordeaux blends, Shiraz (Syrah) is now immensely fashionable as a single varietal. These can be rich and spicy and dry—even the cheapies. The quality of the fruit now emerging is unbelievably good. Watch out Australia. Pinks are also made—these are usually straightforward hammock wines for summer garden sipping.

♟ Rosca Shiraz

♟♟ Adiseno Shiraz Reserve • Bright Bros. Barrica Reserve Shiraz

Tempranillo The Spanish Rioja grape. A couple of years ago Argentinian Tempranillos were soft, juicy, undemanding things, but are now transmogrifying into rich, meaty, dense reds with gamey chocolate notes—a long way from the oak and strawberries of Spain. Some are still a little on the weedy side, others pastille-fruited and faintly earthy. Ripe fruit, lively freshness and flecks of spice in the mass-market Temps make them ideal food reds.

♟ Santa Julia Tempranillo • Corazon Tempranillo

♟♟ Anubis Tempranillo • Zohar Mendoza Tempranillo • Santa Julia Tempranillo Reserve • Q Tempranillo, Zuccardi

Other Reds Pinot Noir makes limited appearances and doesn't yet offer any reason for sleepless nights in Burgundy, being generally cherryish, plummy and softly earthy. No one else yet does Privada like the dry, stylish Norton wine. Watch out for more experimental Spaniards and Italians as Argentina grows in confidence.

RED BLENDS
🍷 Casa Latina Shiraz Tempranillo • Martins Andino Malbec Bonarda • Santa Julia Bonarda Sangiovese • Adiseno 🍷🍷 Cabernet Sauvignon Shiraz • Carrascal, Cave de Weinert

AUSTRALIA

In the last edition the big Australian story was the shortage of wine and their mad scramble to get new vineyards planted. Now those reds are coming on stream at last. Apparently there is a wine glut, though it is hard to believe considering the steady rise in prices. The UK is still Australia's biggest export market (in fact they now buy more Australian wine than French), but now Aussie wine is huge in the USA (so much cheaper than California wine) and things have already got to the point where lots of the good stuff goes direct to the States, bypassing the U.K. completely. Which is annoying, frankly. Where's the loyalty?

Prices are creeping ever upward. Greed, or merely supply and demand forcing up the cost? A bit of both probably, though a risky strategy with countries like Argentina breathing down their necks.

Australia is just going into an interesting second phase. Having made a load of money in the last 15 years, they now have the expertise and resources to take stock, to develop, replant and reposition themselves in the marketplace. The big story now is that Australian winemakers are looking to Europe, and particularly to France, for new (i.e., old) ways of doing things. This is a delicious irony: while the French are scrabbling to introduce more New World methods (stainless steel vinification for intense fruit flavors), the Aussies are looking for inspiration in the French concept of *terroir*. *Terroir*, in other words the earth, stones, aspect to the sun, irrigation—everything that makes that particular spot a vine is planted produce the fruit and the wine it does—has long been a French obsession, and is now fast becoming an Australian one. New vineyards are being planted according to the particular soil, slope and microclimate, and new areas developed specializing in particular grapes. It might even end in the development of formal appellations, such as Goulburn Valley Marsanne and Eden Valley Riesling already enjoy, albeit informally. Having thoroughly cracked the mechanics of good, sound, fruity wine, Australians are now looking for something extra, some personality. There is a feeling that if the *terroir* is taken care of, a very individual character can be developed for individual wines, and, more importantly, can be marketed as such. At first Australian producers were content to make table wine. It was good fruity table wine of high quality, but table wine nonetheless. Now they see that their best wine is of world class, and can command high prices. They not only want the cash, they want the status that goes along with that. So they are now beginning to experiment with ways of giving their wine a bit more of an individual twist. This might even mean, in some cases, abandoning the stainless steel . . . more than one Aussie winemaker has spoken of their attempts to "dirty up" their wine a little.

The big producers like Penfolds and Hardys still dominate wine production and exports, but the vogue is now for little "boutique" wineries, some of them so small they are the result of one man's obsession and a small patch of ground. If that sounds a bit like Burgundy, the comparisons don't end there. It is now also becoming more common to buy in other people's grapes to make wine, not only from across the valley, but also, routinely, from across the state line. There is a famously obsessive winemaker who operates out of a tiny industrial unit on a dockside, and doesn't own any ground at all. There are now well over 1000 wineries in Australia, which may sound like a lot, but is only half as many as in Argentina.

As far as wine trends are concerned, Chardonnay still rules the whites, but is now facing stiff competition from some fascinating rivals. Australia's love of "fusion" cooking, using Asian ingredients, means whites with more sweetness, waxier textures and spice are in vogue. Riesling is very hot, now that very cool vineyards sites are being successfully developed. Sauvignon Blanc is also trendy, and is beginning to find its niche, in newish zones like Adelaide Hills in South Australia, and Margaret River in Western Australia. Margaret River is altogether hugely fashionable and has brought the humble Verdelho grape from Portugal into prominence. Semillon is also in the ascendant, while Colombard and Chenin are on the downturn. Pinot Gris is beginning to appear now, and Viognier has really taken off. On the red wine front, Shiraz is still the most planted variety, and like Cabernet Sauvignon is developing a region by region, hillside by hillside map of styles and flavors that is now reflected in better, more interesting bottle labeling. Cabernet Shiraz blends are still popular, as are Rhône-inspired Grenache blends, but there is now more interest and more kudos in single varietals. Grenache is huge, Merlot on the up though still difficult, and Pinot Noir not cracked yet, though they struggle on. A serious flirtation is now under way with Mediterranean varieties from Spain, Italy, and the South of France.

Drink most Australian wine young and fresh unless advised otherwise or unless it's a serious fine wine with a life in bottle ahead. Fine Shiraz and Cabernet Sauvignon improve in bottle, as do top quality Rieslings, Semillons, even some Chardonnay. Mid- and bargain-priced wine has a tendency to collapse after three or four years, so don't imagine that any dusty leftover 1996s are going to be great. They might be, but then again they might have turned into goo, all tannins deserted, okay for ice-cream sauce but not much else. Having said that, even cheap oaked-Chardonnay benefits from a year in bottle to let the wood soften out.

VINTAGES

2000 was a difficult year, with bad harvest weather and a crop lower in quantity than hoped for. Quality was reasonable to excellent from the salvaged fruit: Sauvignon Blancs are excellent. It was a particularly good year for Hunter Valley, Coonawarra, and for Western Australia. 1999 was supposedly difficult too but wines are delicious. '98 was a cracker: as is the way of these things the final year of a trio of good vintages—'97 and '96 were also good in general. 1995 was pretty bad, as was '93; '94 down in quantity but good in quality. 1990 was an excellent year for long-lived reds.

WHITES

Chardonnay There are fewer big oaky monsters about now, and at the quality end, more elegance. Vivid fruit flavors are still key in the mid-priced range though there is more finesse here too. Thanks to the Chardonnay lake, there is more good stuff at $8 than in recent years. At this price level wines fall into two camps— full-on fruity and tropical (Jindalee) or unexpectedly rich and creamy, yet refined (Normans). There's also lots more cheap stuff that, following the same divide, comes up fruit-juicy and dull, or over-wooded and dehydrating.

🍷 Coldridge Estate Chardonnay • Kilawarra Chardonnay • Banrock Station Chardonnay • Deakin Estate Chardonnay

• Jindalee Chardonnay, Murray-Darling • Lindemans Cawarra Chardonnay • Normans Unwooded Chardonnay • Oxford Landing Chardonnay • Pendulum Chardonnay

🍷🍷 Lindemans Limestone Coast Chardonnay • Penfolds Koonunga Hill Chardonnay • Pirramimma Hillview Chardonnay, McLaren Vale • Woolshed Chardonnay, Coonawarra • D'Arenberg Olive Grove Chardonnay • Tatachilla Chardonnay • Yalumba Barossa Chardonnay • Rosemount Chardonnay • Wolf Blass Barrel Fermented Chardonnay • Bethany Chardonnay, Barossa • Capel Vale Unwooded Chardonnay

🍷🍷🍷 Wirra Wirra Oaked Chardonnay • Wolf Blass President's Selection Chardonnay • Voyager Chardonnay, Margaret River

Chenin Blanc Struggling to find its niche. Difficult to find good ones that avoid being merely appley and dull. Many growers have taken heed from South Africa's Chenin plight and abandoned this variety. There may be a future ahead for Loire-style sweet

Chenins. Meanwhile Western Australia is having a go so it may be too soon to write off this variety just yet (*see* **Verdelho**).

🍷🍷 Capel Vale Chenin Blanc

Colombard Okay in Chardonnay blends but not much used singly and rarely worth the price of admission.

Gewürztraminer Traditionally more of a New Zealand thing but Australian vineyards are currently in "Anything Kiwis do, we can do better" mode and are having a go. Watch this space.

Marsanne A Rhône variety enjoying a mini revival though it has been somewhat eclipsed by Semillon and Verdelho. Still a Victorian specialty though also made in the Hunter Valley. Can be nutty, grassy, waxy and elegant. Some Australian examples bring out hints of strawberry and lime-flavored dryness.

🍷 Cranswick Oak Aged Marsanne

🍷🍷 Barramundi Marsanne • Chateau Tahbilk Unwooded Marsanne

Pinot Gris Ever so trendy, becoming a South Australian specialty. Hip winery Nepenthe is leading the way. Lean fresh fruit, aromatic, spicy, dry, good with food.

🍷🍷 Charleston Pinot Gris, S. Australia (Nepenthe) • Nepenthe Pinot Gris, Adelaide Hills

Riesling Hugely fashionable and in the ascendant.

Some are restrained, minerally, flinty and elegant, others more piquantly fruity, sour sweet with tangy acidity. Most repay a few years in a bottle. The Clare and Eden Valleys in South Australia are still officially the best Riesling sites but Western Australia is producing some stunning wine. Most is at the $12 level and above.

🍷 Samuels Bay Riesling • Wynns Coonawarra Riesling
🍷🍷 Bethany Riesling • Peter Lehmann Riesling • Lindemans Botrytis Riesling • Knappstein Riesling, Clare Valley • Wakefield Riesling, Clare Valley • Capel Vale Riesling, Western Australia • Pewsey Vale Riesling, Eden Valley • Tim Adams Riesling • Alkoomi Frankland River Riesling • Glenara Organic Dry Riesling, Adelaide Hills

Sauvignon Blanc Cool-site vineyard darlings Adelaide Hills and Margaret River (as well as the less obvious Coonawarra) are showing the enormous potential for

Oz Sauvignon. Like Riesling, very fashionable, and being gobbled up by Chardonnay-jaded palates. Most is at the $12 and above level. It's worth it. Watch out Sancerre. But there are also good Sauvignons emerging at the $8 level. Oxford Landing's wine benefits from extended maceration on skins for body and weight, and has classic cut grass, green pepper and lemon flavors.

🍷 Oxford Landing Sauvignon Blanc

🍷🍷 Alkoomi Sauvignon Blanc, Western Australia •
Nepenthe Vineyards Sauvignon Blanc, Adelaide Hills

🍷🍷🍷 Amberley Estate Sauvignon Blanc, Margaret River •
Katnook Sauvignon Blanc, Coonawarra

Sauvignon Semillon For a little more fat tropical fruit perhaps, to add to that steely Sauvignon, or to add a waxy, nutty element and creamy texture. Becoming another Western style though Easterners can also pull it off.

🍷🍷 Tatachilla Sauvignon Semillon, McLaren Vale • Capel Vale Sauvignon Semillon, Western Australia • Brokenwood Cricket Pitch Sauvignon Semillon, South East Australia • Brookland Verse One Sauvignon Semillon, Margaret River • Cape Mentelle Semillon Sauvignon, Margaret River

"...rich and fat, dry and creamy, subtle and delicious. Like spicy lemon curd."

Semillon At last, a white that isn't being dominated by Margaret River or Adelaide Hills. Peter Lehmann's Barossa Semillon (a bargain at $9) is the classic, rich and fat, dry and creamy, subtle and delicious. Like spicy lemon curd. Semillon is everywhere now, whether alone or in blends with Sauvignon or Chardonnay. As well as the rich Barossa version, there's a leaner more European style. It comes in oaked and unoaked versions and can age very well.

🍷 Cranswick Unwooded Semillon, Griffith

🍷🍷 The Barossa Semillon, Peter Lehmann • Basedow Semillon, Barossa Valley • Maglieri Semillon • Penfolds Old Vine Semillon, Barossa Valley • Annie's Lane Semillon, Clare Valley • Rosemount Semillon • McLeans Farm Semillon • Tim Adams Semillon • The Willows Semillon

🍷🍷🍷 Cranswick Botrytis Semillon, Griffith • Nepenthe Lenswood Semillon • Tyrrell's Semillon

Semillon Chardonnay A popular combo at the value end. Good reliable barbecue white.

🍷 Barramundi Semillon Chardonnay • Hardys Chardonnay Semillon

🍷🍷 Ironstone Semillon Chardonnay, Margaret River

Verdelho Suddenly very popular. The previous edition of this guide wrote Verdelho off as a dull white Madeira grape useful for blending but otherwise dreary. . . . How times change! Verdelho has classic Australian attributes, growing waxy and full in the sun, but retaining lots of fresh acidity and hints of spice. Western Australia has shown what can be done and the Eastern States are now following thick and fast. Expect a small explosion here.

🍷🍷 Rothbury Verdelho, Hunter Valley • Capel Vale Verdelho,

Western Australia • Chapel Hill Verdelho, McLaren Vale

Viognier Anything the Rhône can do, Australia can also do, it seems. New release Viogniers are starting to excite Australians, who are buying in quantity; the leftovers are trickling abroad.

♈♈ Oxford Landing Viognier
♈♈♈ Yalumba Eden Valley Viognier • Heggie's Viognier

Sweeties Big sticky yummy things for taking on a spoon when a bit poorly.

♈♈ Brown Bros. Orange Muscat & Flora • Campbells Rutherglen Muscat (fortified)

White Blends Houghton's wine name is shortened for export—we couldn't call it White Burgundy over here. Nor is it Burgundy-like, but it is very tasty nonetheless.

♈♈ Bethany The Manse, Semillon Riesling Chardonnay • Houghton HWB, Western Australia

REDS

Cabernet Sauvignon There are fewer Cabernet bargains than of yore and there's quite a lot of dull stuff at the $8 level. Supermarket own brands are the best bet at this price point. Try also the mass-market brands Hardys and Penfolds. In general, though, Cabernet Sauvignon/Shiraz blends are better at the $8–$9 level. The really good stuff doesn't emerge till $11+.

🍷🍷 Bleasdale Mulberry Tree Cabernet Sauvignon • E&C Cabernet Sauvignon, McLaren Vale • Wakefield Cabernet Sauvignon • Wrattonbully Cabernet Sauvignon, Limestone Coast • Peter Lehmann Cabernet Sauvignon, Barossa • Pirramimma Cabernet Sauvignon, McLaren Vale

Cabernet Shiraz Better than straight Cabernet at the under $9 level (and above, actually, in many cases), with more fruit, spice, structure and oomph. Cabernet Shiraz, a Bordeaux-Rhône hybrid unthinkable in France, has now replaced Aussie "claret" as the nation's favorite blended red.

🍷 Coldridge Estate Shiraz Cabernet • Deakin Estate Shiraz Cabernet
🍷🍷 Oxford Landing Cabernet Shiraz • Elderton Tantalus Shiraz Cabernet, Barossa • Hardys Nottage Hill Cabernet Shiraz • Rosemount Shiraz Cabernet • Saltram Mamre Brook Cabernet Shiraz • Saltram Stonyfell Metala Shiraz Cabernet

Grenache Straight Grenache is on a roll. Chunky, fleshy, raspberryish reds, perhaps spicy, a little savory, with firm but friendly tannins. Australia is still getting to grips with this Rhône Valley Shiraz sibling but it will get there. Has a tendency to the soupy, with overbaked, roasted fruit. Some of the better wines go for a rich full-on style with high alcohol levels and a deep satisfying berry sweetness.

🍷🍷 Mount Hurtle Bush Vine Grenache • Bethany Grenache, Barossa • Normans Old Vine Grenache

Mataro Australian name for Mourvèdre, also from the Rhône. Popular in Shiraz/Grenache blends but seldom seen as a single varietal . . . yet.

Merlot Still not a big Australian variety, which is surprising considering Chile's success. Useful in taming hard, leafy Cabernet Sauvignons in classic "claret" blends, but hasn't taken off yet as a single varietal. Has a tendency to turn soupy and overcooked, though the good'uns have a leathery bucket to pour all that jammy fruit into. Deakin is one of the best at under $9.
🍷 Yellowtail Merlot
🍷🍷 Deakin Estate Merlot • Yalumba Barossa Merlot

Pinot Noir Increasingly fashionable, but still patchy at best, although Adelaide Hills and Tasmania seem to have cracked it (albeit at $12+). Patchy is a euphemism—most Aussie Pinot Noir is pretty dire. A notoriously tricky grape, it stubbornly refuses to enjoy Australia's gorgeous climate and smile in the sun, preferring the cold and rain of Burgundy (and New Zealand? And California? Hmmm. Odd).
🍷🍷 Ninth Island Pinot Noir, Tasmania • Charleston Pinot Noir, Adelaide Hills

Shiraz Australia's national red, planted by immigrants in the Barossa and Eden Valleys in the 19th century and undervalued for a long time. Old vine plantings are now treasured and trendy. France's Syrah grape develops real intensity and personality here, perhaps with spice, liquorice and rich gamey flavors to add to the deep, divine fruit. Still the most planted grape variety, still immensely popular. Superb in blends too. Some individual, boutique-made, fine wine Shiraz tends to the big beefy monster in character, though there are now fewer wines you can stand a stick up in than previously. Not many bargains—expect to pay $10–15.

🍷 Woolpunda Shiraz
🍷🍷 Wirrega Vineyards Shiraz, Limestone Coast • Peter Lehmann Shiraz, Barossa • Pirramimma Stocks Hill Shiraz, McLaren Vale • Wynns Coonawarra Shiraz • Haselgrove Bentwing Shiraz • Oomrah Shiraz, McLaren Vale • Rosemount Shiraz • Annie's Lane Shiraz, Clare Valley • Tim Adams Shiraz • Evans & Tate Shiraz, Margaret River
🍷🍷🍷 Penny's Hill Shiraz, McLaren Vale • Rothbury Brokenback Shiraz • Rufus Stone Shiraz, McLaren Vale

Shiraz Grenache Delicious southern Rhône-style blends, given a solar-powered kick.

♟♟ Tatachilla Grenache Shiraz • Ironstone Shiraz Grenache, Margaret River • D'Arenberg d'Arrys Original, McLaren Vale

Other Red blends Aussie claret was once important (try Smithbrook's sublime example, $13) but recently has been eclipsed by Rhône blends. Wirra Wirra vineyard has perfected the unorthodox Grenache-Shiraz-Cabernet mix. Australians will try anything once.

♟♟ Wirra Wirra W2 Grenache Shiraz Cabernet • Wirrega Cabernet Sauvignon Petit Verdot, Limestone Coast • Woolshed Cabernet Shiraz Merlot • Knappstein Cabernet Merlot • Wirra Wirra Church Block (Cabernet Shiraz Merlot) • Smithbrook Cabernet Sauvignon, Cabernet Franc, Petit Verdot

♟♟♟ Leasingham Cabernet Malbec

NEW SOUTH WALES

Hunter Valley Old established wine region, once spoken of as the only real threat to Barossa. Now left way behind in volume terms, but in quality it can still cut the mustard. Hunter Valley Chardonnay (from Rosemount) pretty much started the New World wine revolution single-handedly in Britain. Rosemount and Rothbury are the best known Hunter Valley producers here. Lots more New South Wales wine appears under vague "South East Australia" labels.

The traditional, original Hunter Valley vineyards are

in a hot, humid zone, but with lots of rain. Whites can be over-ripe and blowsy. This also contributes to the sometimes animal, sweaty notes in the famously leathery, cedar-wooded Hunter Shiraz. But New South Wales is also capable of making superb Marsannes and Semillons.

Cowra Newish, promising district with warm seasons and good irrigation. Outsiders are moving in to develop parcels of land, especially for Chardonnay, and some Shiraz.

Mudgee Hillside vineyard-based with a cooler microclimate than the Hunter Valley. Most grapes are trucked off for winemaking elsewhere. Good Cabernet Sauvignon and Shiraz fruit.

Murumbidgee irrigation area/Griffith Huge tract of irrigated land set up for mass production. A staggering 15% of the total Australian crop is grown here.

Orange Cool-microclimate vineyard area set up to make European styles.

Riverina Still under-exploited area with great potential. Cranswick is the leading winery. The humid climate yields botrytised grapes ideal for dessert wines.

GRAPE VARIETIES
WHITES

Chardonnay Hunter Valley Chardonnay was the original Australian export. In general they still favor that big, toasty, oaky, fruity style, perhaps with cashew nut and yeast character. Rosemount still follows this lushly heavyweight model but Rothbury goes for a leaner, more elegant character and other wineries are following suit. Elegance is now the fashion in Australia and for export and Hunter Valley is having to adjust.

Marsanne A Victoria specialty but good Marsannes also come out of Hunter Valley. Cranswick's $8 wine is rich and creamy, outstanding for the price.

Semillon Fat, fresh, creamy, ripe, yet dry at the finish: Hunter Valley Semillons might be ice creamy, or else yeasty and apple pudding-like, with greengage fruit, like Rosemount's example. Cranswick make a classic sweet (botrytis) Semillon in Griffith, as well as an unwooded $8 bargain. Tyrell's single vineyard Semillons are worth seeking out.

Verdelho Richmond Grove's is typical in its blowsy eastern states apricot ripeness, reined in by tangy acidity.

REDS

Cabernet Sauvignon Rosemount's wine is typical in its full-throttle autumn fruits style, brambly and suffused with porty alcohol. These rich sweet reds can sometimes lack tannin and structure. They taste old-fashioned.

Shiraz Dense cassis and plum fruit, rich lushness, liqueur-style alcohol and a meaty ("horse blanket") character are the trademarks of Hunter Valley Shiraz. Wines are generally plummier and rounder than the blackcurrant-drenched Barossa variety. Cheaper ones are soft, brambly and peppery. Wyndham's wines are big plummy peppery monsters. Rothbury's Broken-back Shiraz is typical: rich and spicy, smoky, a little earthy, with a deep reservoir of black cherry fruit. Old-fashioned is still good in this case.

SOUTH AUSTRALIA

In wine terms, the big region. Almost everything well known turns out to be from here, or from a company based here; 60% of Australia's wine output is South Australian. Lots of "independent" labels turn out to be owned by someone else.

Adelaide Hills Comparatively young vineyard area, founded by Petaluma, who were looking for a cooler microclimate for their whites. Adelaide Hills Chardonnays are of just the right elegant, crisp style to benefit from the fashion for leaner whites. Excellent Rieslings and Sauvignon Blancs. Lenswood, in the heart of the Hills, is the hot (or rather cool) new appellation; überhip winery Nepenthe are based here.

Barossa Valley Still the nerve center of Australia's wine business: most Australian wine still journeys to the Barossa at some point in its production. It's also fertile territory for takeover battles. These big corporations take a lot of their fruit from elsewhere. BRL Hardy, Orlando, Peter Lehmann and the ubiquitous Southcorp (Penfolds) are here. Southcorp are the biggest—they also own Lindemans, Kilawarra, Seppelt, Wynns and Coldstream Hills, but unlike most giant companies, still manage to make products of good quality. Some of their wines are outstanding for the money. They also own Grange, Australia's most fêted red, currently retailing in the U.K. at $150 a bottle.

Barossa Barossa has had its ups and downs; a few years ago it had suffered a nose dive in quality, partly to do with all the corporate activity and branding going on here. The Barossa revival has brought boutique wineries and individualistic wines to the fore. Peter Lehmann has been instrumental in the revival—his Cabernet Sauvignon, Shiraz and Semillon are benchmarks of their styles and seldom beaten for value.

Barossa has become a superb Semillon zone and is improving for reds. Elderton Shiraz is a high class Barossa ambassador with a vividly rich and spicy personality. Bethany is good for whites and for Grenache.

Clare Valley Varied and versatile, with its own cool uplands and warmer valley areas. It's generally a hot dry region, but the hills provide the cooler sites. These hillside vineyards have become synonymous with outstanding Riesling—Eden Valley is the only rival. Wines are for drinking now but also keep well. Good Chardonnays too, and Oz Clarets—Cabernet Merlot blends.

Coonawarra A narrow strip, only about nine miles long and a mile wide, of famously good vineyard soil, which is red and overlays limestone rock. Hectare for hectare, Australia's most profitable red wine zone. Household names, all keen for a piece of the action, are packed in like sardines. Coonawarra Cabernet Sauvignons are still given snob status (though the difference in price may be the only thing you can detect). Also outstanding Shiraz and big beefy red blends.

Eden Valley A historically important wine-making area, though it's only a young appellation, demarcated from the neighboring Barossa Valley because of its distinctive cool climate. Henschke, by local standards a really old vineyard, was one of the founding members of the South Australia wine tradition. Superb Rieslings, rivaled only by those of Clare. Good Chardonnays too. Some expensive reds are made on these high cool slopes.

Langhorne Creek Newish appellation. Bleasdale are here.

Limestone Coast Newish appellation, taking in Coonawarra and Padthaway.

McLaren Vale A varied climate and geography, some parts on higher terrain, some more open to cooling sea winds, make for an interesting and varied wine range. Every conceivable grape variety, red and white, excels here. An outstanding Shiraz area, though (criminally) some venerable old vineyards have been sacrificed to the urban sprawl of Adelaide. Heathcote, a trendy subregion, is good for reds—try the outstanding Rufus Stone Shiraz ($18).

Padthaway (Limestone Coast) Good whites, as well as an important source of fizz grapes for big concerns like Seppelt. Lindemans and Hardys also have vineyards here, whilst companies like Penfolds and Orlando buy grapes to take away. Padthaway Chardonnays were the top snob white five years ago but now appear to have been eclipsed by Adelaide Hills and Western Australia.

Riverland A Murray River irrigation project that's considerably boosted the local crop. Output is dominated by the cheap and cheerful, boxed and table wine market, mostly but not entirely white. Hardys and Angove's are the two big producers.

GRAPE VARIETIES
WHITES

Chardonnay Despite the fashion for leaner, more restrained Chardonnay, tropical, fruit-salad types still exist, and some overdo the malolactic effect, with rather sickly pineapple, coconut and butter. Padthaway wines can be reserved and elegant, or waxy and honey-suckly, their lush creaminess cut through with cool acids. The heat of Coonawarra can make for spicy, intense quince and apricot Chardonnays. Wirra Wirra in McLaren Vale make a low-yield, 60% barrel- and 40% vat-fermented wine with a rich creamy texture and an exotic fruit, cashew nut character. Good wine comes out of Coonawarra, Barossa and Limestone Coast, but the most sought after is from Adelaide Hills. Penfolds and Co. make decent mass-market Chardonnay.

Pinot Gris Nepenthe have taken up this lean, aromatic, spicy variety. Others will follow.

Riesling The Clare and Eden Valleys make delicious, crisp, fruity Rieslings. Generally they're more lime and lemony from Clare, and more all-round fruity and zingy from Eden. Wynns Coonawarra Riesling is lusher, more Chardonnay-like in texture, but with good Riesling acidity. Some botrytis Riesling is also made.

Sauvignon Blanc Australian Sauvignon was too rich and ripe for a long time; it had the right green fruit and sour-sweet complexity, but also too much fat overbaked Oz fruit for true varietal style. Things have changed in the last couple of years though, and Adelaide Hills leads the way. Nepenthe's very well reviewed Sauvignon ferments 15% of the wine in French oak and the remainder in stainless steel, for a style that has some richness and complexity, but still zings with tangy acidity.

Semillon Honeyed, creamy and fat with a flourish of alcohol, and concentrated tangy fruit. Flavors can embrace peach and melon, with herbaceous, lime-fruit complexity and a drying finish. They are the fruitiest of Australia's many fine Semillons. Peter Lehmann's classic wine has lemon curd, cream soda and spice. Semillon blends are also good, typically with Chardonnay. Try the McLaren Vale wine from Tatachilla.

> "Flavors can embrace peach and melon, with herbaceous, lime-fruit complexity..."

Semillon Blends Cheap Semillon Chardonnays can be thin and tropical, with dollops of toasted oak propping up the slender fruit. Better-made examples bring a lovely ripe creaminess to a fresh Chardonnay style. Penfolds' commercial but tasty Rawsons Retreat Semillon/Chardonnay/Colombard has honeyed pear and melon flavors and a slurpable off-dry style.

Verdelho Good examples of this newly fashionable grape can be found at Chapel Hill and Rothbury.

REDS

Cabernet Sauvignon Good cheap Cabernets are hard to find, but South Australia leads the Australian Cabernet race. Peter Lehmann (him again) makes a Cabernet with rich, deep chocolate and leather for $12. This is the price of good modern Cabernet. Some wines still suffer from overcomplication, too sweet and soupy, overdosing on vanilla, though notably fewer than two years ago. Producers are now aiming for a more elegant, more European style with finely balanced fruit, oak and tanin.

Cabernet Sauvignon/Shiraz A true Aussie speciality, sweet with ripe fruit, rich and dry, perhaps with cherry tomato and roasted red pepper flavors. Some are intense with dark blackcurrant and soft plum fruit; others real smoothies, fairly light and mellow with a friendly dollop of oak and vanilla.

Cabernet Blends Good Cabernet Merlots are ripe but

dry, rich but soft, perhaps faintly pastilley, and with plenty of vanilla oak. Some are coffeeish. They tend to be fruitier and sweeter than their cousins in Bordeaux, though some have claret echoes, of tobacco, mint and green pepper. Cabernet Malbecs should have more smoky, savory character.

Grenache Australia has embarked on a real love affair with varietal Grenache, and with Shiraz/Grenache Rhône Ranger reds. Pure Grenache can shine here like almost nowhere else on earth (except Spain perhaps), making delicious, soft wines suffused with spicy fruit and genteelly rough edges.

Shiraz The Australian grape of grapes, nowhere more classic than in South Australia, where France's Syrah variety is transformed into something seductively, densely blackcurrant, perhaps with sappy green edges (salsa, lime and tomato in Coonawarra), Parma violet, chocolate, and a firmly drying finish. Some are so rich you could drape ice cream with them. Others are vacuously soft, muddy with vanilla. Most top flight South Australian Shiraz is now well over $15. Makers create a mystique around their wines and are happy to sell in limited quantity. But there's still plenty of very decent wine under $15.

TASMANIA

A little island making a big impact. Tasmanian wine is increasingly fashionable, thanks to the extraordinary

Dr. Andrew Pirie and his Ninth Island vineyard. Wines are fairly expensive, restrained and elegant. He's especially fêted for his Pinot Noir, an achievement many bigger players on the mainland have thus far failed to pull off.

VICTORIA

Victorian vineyards were decimated by the dreaded phylloxera early this century, but are now almost fully recovered. Some of the most exciting 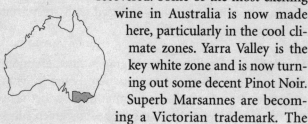 wine in Australia is now made here, particularly in the cool climate zones. Yarra Valley is the key white zone and is now turning out some decent Pinot Noir. Superb Marsannes are becoming a Victorian trademark. The liqueur muscats of Rutherglen are the champion stickies of the continent.

Bendigo Badly phylloxera-hit, but now back in the game thanks to judicious replanting. Some outstanding reds.

Geelong Makes the most of a cool microclimate but also specializes in rich, concentrated reds.

Glenrowan-Milawa Brown Brothers are here, and also Baileys, famous for their sticky, seductive liqueur muscats and big reds.

Goulburn Valley The most respected part of the Central Victoria zone, with the emphasis on quality. Mitchelton (Mitchell) are here. A famous Marsanne area.

Great Western Home to mass market fizz-maker, Seppelt: the wine in all those $8 bottles of private-label sparkling Aussies.

Mornington Weekend playground for the Melbourne rich. Boutique vineyards make some excellent (and high-priced) wines in a cool, sea-breezy maritime microclimate.

Pyrenees Central Victorian hillside vineyards make herby, sturdy reds and some good Chardonnays.

Rutherglen A bakingly hot area in the north east of the state, home to the Australian fortified wine tradition. Morris, Campbells, and Stanton & Killeen make rich, syrupy, heady liqueur muscats. Port-style reds are another local speciality.

Yarra Valley Victoria's trumpcard in the quality race. The fashion for more European, subtler, crisper whites has made Yarra Chardonnays much sought after. Some glorious reds are also emerging: Yarra Valley Pinot Noirs are deeply hip and are sometimes even worthy of the hype.

GRAPE VARIETIES
WHITES

Chardonnay Victorian Chardonnay is rather fine and elegant. Deakin is a good budget brand; Preece has just enough acid to lighten its rich buttery fruit, but a rather aristocratic air nonetheless, and Yarra Valley is in a class of its own.

Marsanne Goulburn Valley Marsannes are among the finest on the continent. Like a Chardonnay kissed by the Riesling fairy, Mitchell Marsanne is initially fat and creamy, before turning sharp, lemony and perfumed. These Marsannes achieve richness but remain bone dry to the end. Just like a good Riesling.

Riesling The voluptuous sweetness and orange citrus tang of Brown Bros. Late Harvest is from a different viticultural planet to the scintillating sherbet-dip character of the Yarra Valley wine.

Sauvignon Yarra Valley Sauvignons tend to be fuller-bodied, fruitier numbers than their Old World relatives. Pyrenees is the up and coming Sauvignon zone.

Stickies Liqueur Muscats are a true Victorian specialty, made from the Brown Muscat grape, a cousin of the premier Muscat à Petits Grains variety. They would be overwhelming in their densely sticky richness but for the redemptive power of a lovely acid freshness. Nonetheless, they ooze.

REDS

Cabernet Sauvignon Victorian Cabernets can have a refreshingly raspberryish, summer fruits touch, especially from the cool-climate zones, though some intense great whoppers are also made.

Pinot Noir Yarra Valley is the leading light in the process of proving (to New Zealand, among others) that Australia can cut the Pinot mustard. Why is the whole world falling over itself to make these raspberry-fruited, faintly gamey, light fresh reds? At least Yarra also makes good fizz with its crop.

Shiraz Victoria is capable of making excellent, chocolatey, creamy, but also dry Shiraz. It also turns out huge blackcurrant-fruited monsters.

WESTERN AUSTRALIA

Western Australia has risen without trace to become one of the most exciting, unpredictable (and deeply, deeply fashionable) vineyard areas, immensely successful but still with tremendous

untapped capacity. The rate of improvement here is now phenomenal. Winemakers are showing that they can do anything, everything, given the right investment, and time. It's very hot in the more northern zones, but most of the vineyards in the cooler south west enjoy a maritime influence which brings cool nights after the heat of the day. Vineyards go against the Aussie grain by specifying locations to an unusually detailed degree, and have sparked a nationwide trend for *terroir*-consciousness. Western Australia Cabernet Sauvignons and Shiraz—often herbaceous in style—can be excellent but can also be disappointingly closed and underfruited. Western Australia is still working on its reds; this is still overwhelmingly a white wine region. Good, often unusually savory Semillons and Sauvignons, plus Chardonnay, Riesling, Verdelho—it's all fabulous. Individuality, of both wineries and their wines, is the Western Australia trademark. As a result, prices can be higher than for Eastern States wines.

Great Southern A new growing area showing enormous potential. All the Australian classics are being made here, with surprising conviction and class.

Lower Great Southern Another developing wine area. The Great Southern crowd are also pushing the boundaries here.

Margaret River Already considered the premium Western Australia region, Margaret River is now considered by many to be the best wine region on the whole continent. Margaret River's success has been the catalyst for the development of a whole new vineyard culture down in the cooler, wetter southwest corner. Mount Barker is prestigious. Sandalford is here, as are Ironstone, Amberley, and Cape Mentelle, one of the Margaret River pioneers. Penfolds are buying in. A feeding frenzy may follow.

Pemberton A newly planted region and one to watch.

Swan Valley The Perth environs are famously arid and summers are merciless, which originally resulted in big, even soupy, concentrated and dense wines, but efforts to lighten and freshen have been very successful. Houghton is based here, but has access to grapes from all over Western Australia.

GRAPE VARIETIES

WHITES

Chardonnay Western Australia can make monster Chardonnays built like Volvo sedans, with maximum fruit, toffee-fudge sweetness, acidity and oak, but it's also capable of turning out delicate elderflower scented New Wave whites from the cooler vineyard zones. Most exported wines are boutique-made, at boutique prices. Capel Vale's Frederick Chardonnay ($23) is a fine example—opulent, oak-aged, lush and complex.

Chenin This dull workhorse white grape is beginning to show its potential in Western Australian hands. Houghton wines are excellent.

Riesling At Margaret River, Cullen's wine leads the pack, though at a price. Frankland River is becoming a Riesling zone—try Alkoomi's superb wine (around $12). Capel Vale vineyards benefit from sea winds for a long slow ripening period; classic steel and petrol and lime Rieslings are the result.

Sauvignon Western Australian Sauvignon has hit the headlines recently. Comparisons have not only been made with the New Zealand classic style, but also with the flintier, more subtle style of Sancerre itself, back in northern France. Margaret River is the zone and Amberley the vineyard for Sancerre-style wine, at around $15. Alkoomi follows a more flavorful NZ model ($12).

Semillon Western Australian Semillons can be powerful and aromatic, and they age well; Margaret River ones are known for their grassy palate. The tremendously elegant Amberley is world class. Xanadu Semil-

Western   Australia
SEMILLON CHARDONNAY 1997
PRODUCED & BOTTLED BY IRONSTONE VINEYARDS. MARGARET RIVER
750mL. Produce of Australia 13.0%Vol.

lon is made for keeping. Sauvignon Semillons can be excellent too: Brookland Verse One ($12) from Margaret River tastes very expensive indeed. Cape Mentelle, also at Margaret River, makes Sauvignon Semillon a world away from the weedy, obvious wines of South Africa, say. Semillon Chardonnay can also be delicious, lending grassy notes and tropical fruit to the mix—try Ironstone's wine from Margaret River (around $9).

Verdelho Western Australian Verdelho was the spark for the Verdelho revival across the country. Capel Vale's fragrant, tropically ripe yet dry and lemon-fresh wine has been hugely influential.

REDS

Cabernet/Cabernet Blends Warm climate Western Australian Cabernets can be rich, cedar-boxy, spicy, delicately earthy Oz clarets. Margaret River reds are creating a new Cabernet-blend style. Cape Mentelle Cabernet Merlot has ripe red peach-flesh character alongside a light, fruity plum and strawberry palate. There are a fair few duffers about, too: Western Australia is still working on its reds. Some can be too French in style, showing the hard, sappy character of a young Bordeaux.

Shiraz/Shiraz Blends Supple, easy, peppery, spicy Shiraz, perhaps with a herbaceous edge, is becoming a

Western Australian style, though some are ripe and friendly in a faintly vacuous way. Margaret River Rhône-style wines show enormous promise. Ironstone Shiraz Grenache is one of the most successful so far, offering gorgeous fruit and texture for a bargain price ($11). Some straight Shiraz is too tannic and closed up.

CHILE

By any reckoning, Chile is a huge success story. In 1990 the UK imported 215,000 cases of Chilean wine. In 1999 it was up to 4.3 million cases. And still the Chilean vineyards continue to expand, to improve, and plant masses of new vines.

There is good reasoning behind all this. Chile's phenomenal achievement isn't down to snobbery, mystique or the high points given to its wines by dry old academics sitting in committee. Instead, it's down to consumer power. People discovered that here there was world class wine, with fruit unparalleled anywhere—more importantly, here was fruity, sun-drenched, incredibly delicious wine, easy to love, easy to drink, and at very easygoing prices. The thing just went whoosh. Into orbit.

Things have settled out a bit since then. Some producers got greedy and overcropped their fruit; others did wild and ill-considered things with oak; prices rose and quality dipped. Chile was drunk on its own delirious success. Things are improving and evening out again now. Like Australia and South Africa, and to an extent Argentina, boutique wineries—small operations, run with love and with entrepreneurial flair—have risen up and dotted the marketplace with rare, individualistic goodies at high prices. Of these Super-Chileans, Caballo Loco from Valdivieso was the first to go Super, in 1997, electing to go for very low yields and the best possible quality. There is now a clutch of wines retailing at around or over the $30 level. At the other end of the scale, there are still lots of gorgeous wines at $8 and $9, and even below the $8 level. Though it's necessary to shop carefully and stick to trusted names.

The fruit is of an astonishing purity and depth of flavor. The world has taken note of Chilean Cabernets that taste of a kind of deep rich blackcurrant wine, of jammy plummy Merlots with leather and spice, buttery and intensely fruity Chardonnays, and the world has been hugely influenced. The only regret is that so much uniformly delicious international wine is made, at the expense of more indigenous, southern varieties, and at the expense of experimentation. But this, too, is beginning to change as Chile grows in confidence.

Chile is sandwiched between the cold Andes and the chilly Pacific, so despite sitting on a latitude equivalent to Beirut, the climate around Santiago is perfect for vineyards. In addition, the Incas thoughtfully provided a huge network of canals and irrigation systems. Drought occasionally rears its ugly head, and El Niño is infamous for affecting harvests, but otherwise the conditions are as near perfect as anywhere. Ten years ago there was little stainless steel and new French oak in evidence. Now they are the norm and Chile is awash with foreigners, whether flying winemakers passing through or big corporations looking for a piece of the action. Mondavi of California is in Caliterra, the Rothschilds at Los Vacos, and Miguel Torres has a Chilean operation. Dallas-Conte benefits from Australian input, from Oz winery giant Mildara Blass. The 2000 vintage has caused some alarmist panic though, not because of bad weather but because of overproduction. It is said that quantity is being chosen over quality in many areas, which leaves wines dilute and dull. However, the wines are still of fantastic quality for the price overall. There's still no close rival anywhere for the range available at the $8–$10 price level.

It's good to see the grape varieties getting more varied. The Cab-Merlot-Char trinity has been enlivened by the introduction of Sauvignon Blanc in force, as well as Semillon, Viognier, and masses of Gewürztraminer. The good whites are excellent, though few achieve the dizzy quality of the best reds. Cabernet Franc, Carignan, Carmenère and Pinot Noir are growing in number; Malbec and Syrah/Shiraz increasingly important, though Cabernet Sauvignon still rules, with Merlot as deputy. Individual producers are still far more important than region. The concept of *terroir* hasn't really taken off yet. Good new names to look out for include Viña Porta, Terra Mater and, best of them all, Gracia, whose reds have a nostalgic quality, reminiscent of the bargain blockbusters of the mid 1990s.

VINTAGES
2000 is down in quality (even the Chileans describe it as "modest"), nothing like the fabulous '99s and '97s though not as bad as the '98 crop. 1996 was also good. Most reds start to fade away after three or so years, though quality wine can age much longer. Indeed, some now demand aging, made for a prolonged maturity in bottle. In general whites should be drunk young and fresh.

REGIONS

Generally it's too cold and wet in the south and too hot and arid in the far north for viticulture. It hardly ever rains in the **Atacama Desert**. A smallish area surrounding Santiago in the center is responsible for almost all the wine made.

Aconcagua The region divides into Aconcagua Valley, just to the north of Santiago, and Casablanca, a subregion. Aconcagua Valley is hot and arid, a natural reds zone. Errázuriz use cooler hillside vineyard sites for their whites.

Casablanca Valley To the west of Santiago, closest to the Pacific. The traditional white wine region, producing crisp, lemony wines in its cool microclimate, Veramonte and Santa Rita whites among them. Casablanca winery is excellent, as is Concha y Toro. Chardonnays and Sauvignons thrive in these conditions, as do

Gewürztraminer and Viognier. Casablanca is now developing as a Pinot Noir region.

Central Valley Takes in Maipo, Rapel and Curicó. This is a warm, traditionally red wine zone, but good whites are appearing.

Curicó To the north of Maule. Masses of mass market wine as well as some more interesting wineries. Carmen, Errazuriz, Montes, Santa Carolina, Casablanca and others are Curicó-based. Lontue is a sub-region.

Lontue Home of Valdivieso, probably Chile's best winery. Viña San Pedro is also here, making good reds and whites, including supermarket Sauvignons. Santa Carolina makes whites here.

Maipo The Barossa Valley of Chile: the hub of the industry, and virtually part of the eastern suburbs of Santiago. Good reds (some of the biggest), Cabernet Sauvignon-dominated, plus some fine Chardonnay. Concha y Toro rule supreme but others are coming up on the rails. Gracia makes its extraordinary Carmenere Reserve here. Santa Rita and Carmen have vineyards.

Maule Reds mostly better than whites so far, but cool areas are producing good Sauvignon.

Rapel Good solid region with some exciting new producers. Big and versatile, with some particularly good Merlot emerging. La Rosa is here. Good reds from wineries like Casa Lapostolle, Cono Sur, Dallas-Conte, Carmen, Santa Rita and Isla Negra, as well as some whites. Colchagua (Luis Felipe Edwards, Isla Negra) and Cachapoal (La Palmeria, Viña Porta) sub-regions are on the upswing.

Bio Bio An up-and-coming, previously plonk-dominated zone to the south of Maule. Part of the Southern group of appellations. Cono Sur's Gewürztraminer is its best known wine so far.

GRAPE VARIETIES

WHITES

Chardonnay At its best Chilean Chardonnay is superbly well-balanced, richly fruity, brilliantly textured, with good friendly acids, soft tannins and satisfying structure. Some are more tropical, with over-ripe hot region fruit reined in by firm oak. Others are more pared down and modern, with a lemony clean character. In general Chardonnays seem to be getting more creamy and yeasty, as pronounced barrel-fermented character becomes more popular. Casablanca's Santa Isabel Chardonnay is 80% cold-fermented, but 20% oak-made and left on its lees for a creamy rich style and long finish. Caliterra's wine is still good after all these years, for a riper, more tropically fruit-driven style. At the other end of the price spectrum, the attempt to make European style Chardonnays of dis-

tinction and refinement is paying off. Wines like Errazuriz's Reserva and Dallas-Conte's show how classy Chilean Chardonnay can be at even the $9–$12 level.

🍷 La Palmeria Chardonnay • Santa Carolina Chardonnay • Caliterra Chardonnay • Casillero del Diablo Chardonnay • Sierra Los Andes Chardonnay • Isla Negra Chardonnay

🍷🍷 Dallas Conte Chardonnay • Errazuriz Chardonnay • Cono Sur Chardonnay Reserve • Santa Inés Chardonnay Reserve • Castillo de Molina Reserve Chardonnay • Casa Lapostolle Chardonnay • Casablanca Santa Isablel barrel fermented Chardonnay • Errazuriz Chardonnay Reserva • Errazuriz Wild Ferment Chardonnay • Montes Alpha Chardonnay

🍷🍷🍷 Casa Lapostolle Cuvee Alexandre Chardonnay

Chenin Blanc Chilean Chenins can be dry with fragrant pear fruit, or medium sweet and tropical. They rarely shine, and there are fewer available in Britain now than there were three years ago. Wineries are turning to other successful varietals and giving up on dull old Chenin.

Gewürztraminer Chilean Gewürztraminer can be wild and spicy, with over-ripe, overheated grapey fruit,

perfumy character, and a sour-sweet, sour apple and honey palate. The finish can be hard and bitter. But having said that, more and more outstanding cool zone Gewürztraminers are coming out now, and all at low prices. Canepa's is probably the benchmark for quality, showing lots of varietal character and flair. Cono Sur's has more of a Latin feel, with its pear, mango and orange flavors.

🍷 Canepa Gewürztraminer • Cono Sur Gewürztraminer • Sierra Los Andes Gewürztraminer • Undurraga Gewürztraminer
🍷🍷 Carmen Gewürztraminer, Curicó

Riesling Chilean Rieslings tend to be crisp and simple (though others are too soft and ripe) with pear and

apple fruit. Melon notes are usual. Not much movement here. Interest appears to be fizzling out.

Sauvignon Blanc In the past, Sauvignons have tended
to be either tropically crisp, their blowsy ripe fruit balanced by green tangy character, or lean and grapefruity. Originally Chile had a lot of Sauvignonasse and
Sauvignon Vert, the Blanc's inferior cousins, which
didn't help. Now more New Zealand-style Sauvignons
are beginning to appear, with pronounced gooseberry
fruit: 35 South's bargain wine has a grassy herby style
with lovely zingy fruit and a fresh citrus finish; at
under $8 an unbeatable Sauvignon Blanc. Warm
region Sauvignons are still blowsy and over-ripe; look
out for wines from cool climate zones.

♀ Santa Inés Sauvignon Blanc • Carta Vieja Sauvignon
Blanc, Maule • Las Collinas
Sauvignon Blanc, Lontue •
Vistasur Sauvignon Blanc •
35 South Sauvignon Blanc,
Viña San Pedro, Lontue
♀♀ Errazuriz Sauvignon
Blanc, Curicó • Santa Isabel
Sauvignon Blanc • Pirque
Sauvignon Blanc, Maipo

PIRQUE ESTATE
SAUVIGNON BLANC
2000

MAIPO VALLEY
PRODUCT OF CHILE

75 cl e.   RUNABOUT   13.5% vol

PRODUCED AND BOTTLED BY VIÑA HARAS DE PIRQUE
IMPORTED BY MARKS AND SPENCER PLC, BAKER STREET, LONDON, U.K.

Semillon Chilean Semillons can be attractively fresh
and fat, with apricot and custard fruit, but rarely
achieve the complexity of a good Australian example.
Canepa's $6 wine is superb value and really delicious.
♀ Canepa Semillon, Colchagua

Viognier Cono Sur is the name for Chilean Viognier. Handmade with no mechanical crushing involved, this wine is exceptional value for money.
🍷 Cono Sur Viognier, Rapel

REDS

Cabernet Franc Now beginning to appear as a single varietal. Valdivieso's superb wine has set the standard.
🍷🍷 Valdivieso Cabernet Franc Reserve, Lontue

Cabernet Sauvignon Classic Chilean Cabernet Sauvignon is very good indeed, with silky, voluptuous (but also dry) blackcurrant fruit. Some, thanks to new French oak influence, have claret-like echoes of the cigar box, tobacco pouch or fresh mint, with firm subtle tannins and fine structure: these beautifully balanced Bordeaux taste-alikes are now very big business. Others are simpler and sweeter, with blackberries and cream, vanilla and coffee notes and peppery edges. There seems to be more decent $6 and $8 Cabernet about than three years ago. Even some of these cheapies manage to offer rich blackcurrant and spice flavors. Astonishingly, there are Chilean Cabernet vines older than those of Bordeaux.

🍷 La Palmeria Cabernet Sauvignon • Quiltro Cabernet Sauvignon • Casa Leona Cabernet Sauvignon (La Rosa) • 35 South Cabernet Sauvignon • Vistasur Cabernet Sauvignon • Casillero del Diablo Cabernet Sauvignon, Concha y Toro • Isla Negra Cabernet Sauvignon • Terra Mater Cabernet Sauvignon • Valdivieso Cabernet Sauvignon • Viña Porta Cabernet Sauvignon, Maipo

🍷🍷 Castillo de Molina Cabernet Sauvignon Reserva, Lontue • Gracia Pasajero Cabernet Sauvignon • Casa Lapostolle Cabernet Sauvignon, Rapel • Castillo de Molina Reserve Cabernet Sauvignon • Cono Sur Cabernet Sauvignon Reserve, Chimbarongo • Errazuriz Cabernet Sauvignon, Aconcagua • Santa Inés Cabernet Sauvignon Reserve • Santa Rita Cabernet Sauvignon Reserva • Carmen Reserve Cabernet Sauvignon, Maipo • Casa Lapostolle Cabernet Sauvignon • Santa Rita Reserve Cabernet Sauvignon •

Veramonte Cabernet Sauvignon • Dallas-Conte Cabernet
Sauvignon, Rapel

Carmenere This minor Bordeaux claret grape has
been in Chile for a long time, though labelled and used
as Merlot for much of it. Now that the error has come
to light, producers are either carrying on regardless,
saying that Carmenere improves the flavor and texture
of Merlot, or doing as the exciting new winery Gracia
have done and developing the Carmenere as a single
varietal. Their wine is rich, dark and herby, alcoholic
and weighty. Their winemaker hails from the Loire
Valley.

♟♟ Viña Gracia Carmenere Reserve Especial • Apaltagua
Carmenere

Carmenere Cabernet Blends Chilean "Clarets" are
beginning to take off.

♟♟ Santa Inés Cabernet Sauvignon Carmenere Reserva •
Montes Cabernet Sauvignon Carmenere

Malbec Chilean Malbecs can be good, with savory,
tomatoey, smoky fruit and sweet firm ripeness. Cheapies can be harsh and under-ripe. Valdivieso is the name
to go for.

♟♟ Valdivieso Malbec • Valdivieso Barrel Select Malbec

Merlot Chilean Merlots are the best in the world at the
$8 level. No contest. Flavor-wise they vary, perhaps
with a cranberry accent, with cherry, strawberry and
spice, or deeply rich and dark with velvety plum fruit.

Blackcurrants and blackberries often jostle with plum in the good ones, perhaps with a perfumy pastille edge. Some are more savory, with loganberry and mulberry fruit, an herbal edge and an earthy dryness. Casa Lapostolle's Merlot has a juicy ripe style but also cedarwood spice. Sappy green edges and firm oak help firm up the sweeter, juicier Merlots, though there's a tendency lately for over-ripe and gloopy wines which lack enough acid, tannin and shape. Cheap Merlot can be juicy and dull. Mass replantings have introduced more true Merlot: previously there was a lot of Carmenere grown here under the Merlot name. Some producers feel that a Carmenere-Merlot mix is still best.

> "Chilean Merlots are the best in the world at the $8 level. No contest."

🍷 Antares Merlot • Casa Leona Merlot (La Rosa) • Cono Sur Merlot • Las Collinas Merlot • Viña Gracia Merlot, Curioso • Montgras Merlot • La Palmeria Merlot
🍷🍷 Errazuriz Merlot • Valdivieso Barrel Select Merlot • Cono Sur Merlot Reserva • Isla Negra Merlot • Santa Rita Reserva Merlot • Casa Lapostolle Merlot • Carmen Reserve Merlot, Rapel
🍷🍷🍷 Casa Lapostolle Cuvee Alexandre Merlot

Barrel Selection
RESERVE

VALDIVIESO
MERLOT
1999 CHILEAN WINE

Pinot Noir Most is light, faintly gamey, with strawberry and spice. Cono Sur lead the way at the budget end: fruity, simple and delicious. Valdivieso's Pinots are good in a good year. Otherwise there's not a lot to recommend, but Pinot is being worked on very concertedly and should show rapid improvement.

♟ Cono Sur Pinot Noir
♟♟ Cono Sur Pinot Noir Reserve
♟♟♟ Errazuriz Pinot Noir Reserve

Syrah The last edition of the guide said that Syrah/Shiraz was just beginning to be tried. These new plantings are coming online now and showing the potential for Chilean Syrah. More please.

♟♟ Caliterra Syrah • Montgras Single Vineyard Syrah •
Errazuriz Syrah Reserve

FRANCE

Australian wine is getting more French. French wine is getting more Australian. Has the world gone mad? Actually, no. It all makes good sense. There's no doubt that the French have been in a mild state of panic in the last few years. The home market is sobering up. A good deal less rough red wine is downed with lunch. The young people are turning to *bière* en masse. Wines from the New World are beginning to edge into the supermarket wine aisles (though they can't compete on price—French hypermarkets are stuffed to the gunnels with 20 franc red). What worries them most, however, is the preference the big world out there is showing for fruit-driven, sunshine-filled, intensely flavored, easy drinking wine that isn't French in origin. The export market is looking a bit wobbly. The French are taking action.

The results of this action can be seen all over the

country. Loire Sauvignon Blanc is reasserting itself in the face of the fad for New Zealand upstarts. The Rhône is turning out delicious Grenache-Syrah (Shiraz) blends that cock a snook at Australia. As do wines labeled Chardonnay-Bourgogne from Burgundy. Mass market Pinot Noirs are getting fruitier, more Californian in style. The Languedoc is showing that, like McLaren Vale in South Australia, it can make wines of all colors and styles and do them brilliantly at low prices, so there, pah!

Change is happening piecemeal, here and there, depending on the foresight and marketing sense of individual producers and wineries. Even so, there has been some alarm among traditionalists, that traditional French wines are under threat, that they risk being subsumed under a blandly international New World style the world will tire of as fast as it succumbed. This isn't going to happen, though it is most likely to in the South, where the huge, vast Vin de Pays d'Oc region is most open to change and least hidebound by tradition. Those who complain about the loss of the old style of Midi red should be tied to a chair and forced to drink some of that dirty nasty flabby oaky dry old stuff. Besides, there are actually very few southern reds that taste like they could have been made in a stainless steel tank anywhere in the world. There are, admittedly, some. But the Languedoc particularly is still a land of fiercely independent and proud winegrowers with their own ideas and a strong local following.

French winegrowers are also coming to understand

the value of *domaine*-made wine. In the Loire and Burgundy, particularly, there is a move towards making and bottling wine at home, and marketing it as such, rather than selling on wine or fruit to Appellation Contrôlée merchants and co-ops. The system has a tendency towards uniformity, and for centuries French winemakers have striven to make wine in the official style of their own AC, as close to that of their neighbors as possible. Strong regional styles developed in this way. Now, though, more and more producers are recognizing that they can keep their traditions alive while also creating something individual. They can see what a huge success boutique wineries have enjoyed in the New World with their unique wines, personal labels and branding. A bit of this has rubbed off. Much of the best wine currently coming out of France is of traditional stock but has also benefited from a New World education.

AC (Appellation Contrôlée, or AOC, Appellation d'Origine Contrôlée) wines must come from the right strip of land, must be made with certain (traditional) grape varieties, and must be of a certain strength. Added to all of which, there are rules about the vineyard's planting, pruning, and yield. Everything must be done by the book.

VDQS (Vin Délimité de Qualité Supérieure), the quality band in between AC and Vin de Pays, is being phased out.

Vin de Table covers all wine not covered by an AC or by a Vin de Pays Classification. There are few rules, and very little pleasure to be had from drinking them either. Though occasionally good simple wines emerge which have broken all the rules about how a wine is grown and made, so can't be allowed an AC or Vin de Pays status.

Vin de Pays wines are regionally defined. There are some rules, but makers are nothing like as hidebound as producers in AC vineyards are.

VIN DE PAYS

The engine room of the New Wave. Vin de Pays classifications cover all the wine-growing districts of France, but the most impressive are gathered in the south and southwest.

Reds are better than whites—largely because the best areas are traditionally red wine producers—but whites are improving rapidly. Some reds have already become famous and fashionable. Mas de Daumas Gassac, strictly speaking a mere Vin de pays de l'Hérault, has been called the Lafite of Languedoc (and is priced accordingly).

There are now five big Vin de Pays categories thanks to the introduction of a new one, Vin de pays des Portes de Mediterranée in 2000: it covers the three Alpes departments, plus Ardèche, Drome, Var and Vaucluse. Jardin de la France covers the Loire Valley, north and west (see **LOIRE** for wines). The Comté Tolosan covers the west/

southwest corner. Comtés Rhodaniens accounts for the Rhône and eastern side, and the Vin de pays d'Oc covers that great swathe of vineyard land across the south and southwest, the Midi. Vin de Pays d'Oc is easily the most important of all the classifications, in both numbers imported here and quality.

Producers can also use the Département name, like Vin de Pays dù Gard. Or they can use traditional names, like Côtes de Gascogne.

We also see a fair number of Rhône vins du pays—from Coteaux de l'Ardèche, Vaucluse, Principauté Orange and Gard, as well as Languedoc Roussillon favorites like Vin de Pays de l'Aude, de l'Hérault and des Cévennes.

ALSACE

Wine critics may rave about them, but the public is still resistant to the charms of Alsace. Our customary suspicion of German (or German-seeming) wine, with Germanic scripted labels and unknown grape varieties puts a lot of people off. Even those who have been converted to these fantastic, complex wines can be put off buying them. It's so difficult to predict how dry or sweet, fruity or lean, tangy or flinty an unknown bottle will be.

It isn't surprising that wines are more Germanic

than French; Alsace was only returned to French own-
ership at the end of World War I. German grapes are
grown here, but with a French approach, which makes
Alsace-German comparisons fascinating, in wine-tast-
ing terms. Alsace wines have their own inimitable
character, full of old-fashioned charm, perhaps drier
than German wines, and more alcoholic—more of the
sugar is fermented out. The 2000 vintage was the first
to be made under new tighter controls, demanding
lower fruit yields and more sugars in the wine.

Alsace is the only AC allowed to use the grape variety on the label, and it has only been an AC since 1962.
The best wines tend to be varietals, like Riesling and
Gewürztraminer. Other good wines are made, but
Riesling still rules, and rightly so. These are world class
wines, though it's important to pick your producer
carefully. Wines are characteristically both dry and luscious, though a warm summer can produce sweeter
examples. Vintages can show enormous variety. 50
vineyards were awarded Grand Cru status in 1992.

Purposefully   very-rich-and-possibly-also-sweet
wines can be had, labeled Vendange Tardive (late harvest, naturally very sweet) or Sélection de Grains
Nobles (which are botrytised—the fruit is allowed a
controlled level of over-ripeness and rot before picking). Whether very dry or super sweet, Alsace wines are
perfect with food, whether serving as aperitif, main
course or dessert and cheese partner. Their characteristic natural sweetness (which in the best wines is tempered by insistent dryness and piercing acidity) makes
them ideal with Pacific Rim and Fusion cooking. This

is one reason that Riesling has become such a big hit in Australia.

VINTAGES
2000 was good, '99 very mixed, and '98 not classic either. 1997 was good to excellent, '96 pretty good to excellent, '95 low in quantity but of good quality, and '94 like '96. There are still good mature wines available from '88, '89 and '90.

BUYING ALSACE WINES
In Alsace the producer is pretty much all you need to know. Good producers produce good wine, of whatever sort or pedigree. Many bottles are with us only fleetingly, bought in small parcels by wine shops and

merchants, rather than appearing year to year on their shelves. Good names to look out for include: Beblenheim, Bott-Geyl, Hugel, Kuentz-Bas, Albert

Mann, Ribeauville, Rolly-Gassmann, Schoffit, Schlumberger, Trimbach, Turckheim, Weinbach and Zind-Humbrecht. Turckheim is a good Co-Op with a range of wines at low prices that provide a good introductory tour of Alsace. They own 500 hectares of vines around the foothills of the Vosges mountains and are Alsace's biggest exporter to the U.K. At the other end of the price spectrum, the really good stuff can easily cost $40–$53 a bottle or more. These rare wines repay their price by turning into something ambrosial after a period of bottle age.

GRAPE VARIETIES

Auxerrois Ripe and unusual flavors, spicy, even slightly pungent. Often blended with Pinot Blanc.

Edelzwicker Not a grape variety, but a (usually cheap) blend. Often contains Auxerrois, as well as Sylvaner, Pinot Blanc and Chasselas.

Gewürztraminer Luscious Alsace speciality, though it can be bone dry. Rich yet delicate, ripe and exotic, gently spicy and floral. The more expensive, fine wines tend to be rich and unctuous, perhaps with lychee and nut to add to the honey and spice. Despite this they remain fresh with good acidity.

"rich and unctuous ... with lychee and nut to add to the honey and spice."

♟♟ Gewürztraminer, Cave de Ribeauville • Gewürztraminer
Cave de Turckheim • Tesco Finest Alsace Gewürztraminer
♟♟♟ Zind Humbrecht Gewürztraminer • Gewürztraminer
Sonnenglanz, Grand Cru, Bott-Geyl

Muscat Usually Muscat Ottonel, and not Muscat à
Petits Grains or the Alexandrian sort. Should be light
and grapey. Often sweet. Can be good chilled as an
aperitif.
♟♟ Muscat Riquewihr, Bott-Geyl • Muscat vin d'Alsace,
Albert Mann

Pinot Blanc (Klevner) Cheap Pinot Blanc is often
fairly neutral, at worst downright bland. Turckheim's
bargain wine is peachy, spicy, with mineral and yeast
character, lemon and floral notes. Others are apple-
fruity, ripe and creamy.
♟♟ Pinot Blanc Cuvée Réserve, Turckheim
♟♟♟ Pinot d'Alsace, Zind Humbrecht

Pinot Noir Not all the wine made in Alsace is white.
Though most of the good wine is. This wine is unfiltered, which leaves it with a profoundly summery fruit
character.
♟♟ Pinot Noir Bott-Geyl, Beblenheim

Riesling The classic Alsace white. Well-made Rieslings
age well in bottle. Drier than the classic German variety, in fact some have suffered from being over-dry and
austere in the past. Hugel is one of the oldest wine
families in France—they have been making wine since

the 15th century. Bott-Geyl's Zellenberg wine needs time in the cellar to really shine.

♟♟ Bott-Geyl Riesling, Burgreben de Zellenberg • Hugel Riesling

♟♟♟ Riesling Bott-Geyl • Riesling Harth, Schoffit • Zind Humbrecht Riesling, Clos Hauserer

Sylvaner Generally light and insubstantial. Out of fashion.

Tokay Pinot Gris Pinot Gris is known as Tokay-Pinot Gris in Alsace. At its best, aromatic and delicately spicy (even musky), rich and honeyed. At its worst, disastrously flabby. Albert Mann's wine from old vine-stock has lemon, apricot and lime with a dry spice finish, contriving to be both luscious and dry. Zind Humbrecht's wines are blockbusters of flavor and texture.

♟♟ Tokay Pinot Gris, Cave de Ribeauville • Tokay Pinot Gris, Turckheim

♟♟♟ Tokay Pinot Gris Vieilles Vignes, Albert Mann • Tokay Pinot Gris Herrenweg, Zind Humbrecht

BORDEAUX

The claret region—claret being the British term for Red Bordeaux, whether Merlots, Cabernet Sauvignons, or any legally allowed blend of the two, plus Cabernet Franc and lesser grapes like Carmenère, depending on the location and the local regulations.

So diverse a region that it operates like a small country, Bordeaux has around 300,000 acres of vineyards and 24 main ACs, spread out along and around the Dordogne and Garonne valleys in south west France. It's a fact astonishing but true that this one French region makes more wine each year than the entire annual output of Chile and South Africa combined. More than the whole of Australia.

French paranoia about its status in the world of wine is nowhere more deeply felt than here. So they have been making more of an effort to modernize and get their act together for the 21st century, making wine people actually want to drink. There has been a tendency of late to lavish big advertising budgets on their New Wave products before the products are really ready to launch, which is unfortunate. There is still a lot of work to do at the cheap and medium-priced points but progress has been made, particularly in Bordeaux Supérieur, and the satellite ACs like Côtes de Blaye and Bourg, Castillon and Duras. Quality is still patchy, though, even in the expensive wine zones (ESPECIALLY in the expensive wine zones). Many people's bad experience of Bordeaux emanates from one of two things: 1) buying a cheapish bottle with a fancy label—it's bad because it's just bad wine, despite having vineyards in the right AC area, and 2) buying a more expensive bottle with a fancy label, expecting because it's expensive and the name is household, the wine will be sublime, and finding that it's anything but. This is either because it's just bad (*see above*), or more likely, it's nowhere near ready to drink yet, a fact rarely spelled out clearly on the label. "Don't drink this wine before its seventh birthday or it will taste like chewing pencils," would help.

> "Don't drink this wine before its seventh birthday or it will taste like chewing pencils."

The big story this year has been the quality of the 2000 vintage. Is it or isn't it destined for greatness? This is a question with a lot of money riding on it (dollars and yen, mostly) as investors will pay top prices for years they feel confident will be classics. It's a waiting and guessing game—the wine sold En Primeur (direct from being made) won't be ready to drink for years and years and may or may not turn out to be worth its weight in gold. Bordeaux producers have hyped the 2000 vintage, saying it's one of the greats, perhaps even as good as 1961 and 1982. Some critics agree. Some are more guarded in their praise. And others, in Britain particularly, have denounced the whole thing as a PR exercise without any real basis in quality. Certainly the international market has gone bananas for 2000 claret—the vintage is selling for ludicrous prices in barrel, and will be $300 a bottle AT LEAST when it's released in 2003. (Note Bene: We are of course talking about the Fine Wine here, the top classed growths. You will still be able to buy Château de l'Abbaye de St Fermé for around $9).

The Bordeaux focus is overwhelmingly on the reds, but good and interesting whites also come from this region. Plain Bordeaux Blanc is rarely good and should be avoided unless a particular name is recommended. The most reliable white appellation is that of Pessac-Léognan, a gravel-soiled 15 year old sub-region of the better known Graves AC. The sweet whites of Sauternes are internationally loved (and chased after).

People get anxious about whether Bordeaux is ready to drink. Bordeaux Rouge and some other lighter reds need hardly any ageing, in fact are better drunk young and fresh. Ripe and ready Bordeaux Supérieur should be drinkable in two years. Basic clarets are ready in 5–7 years, Cru Bourgeois at 10, and heavyweight First Growths (Premier Crus) may take 20 or 30 years in bottle to reach their peak. Some last much longer.

CRUS AND CLASSIFICATIONS

The claret classification system dates from 1855 and is badly in need of overhauling. It was originally a hastily drawn-up lay guide to the Médoc (plus Haut Brion in the Graves) done for the Paris Exhibition of 1855, so all the listed wines are reds. Graves, Sauternes and St-Emilion (but not Pomerol) were given their own classification systems later, as were Champagne and Burgundy. The label Premier Cru, or First Growth, relates purely to the estate's rank in this 1855 system. There are five "divisions," and below the fifth, Cru Bourgeois (the Highly Commendeds of this particular village show). Some modern Cru Bourgeois wines are easily the equal of their more famous, Growth Status neighbors. The only change made to the 1855 classification took place in 1973 when Mouton Rothschild was promoted to First Growth status.

VINTAGES

2000 was a pretty good year, with good harvest weather for once (other than in Sauternes). A good year for medium priced and cheapish claret. 1999 was mixed, better for Merlot than for Cabernet; '98 better for Merlot too—buy St-Emilion and not Médoc. 1997 was pretty good, but pricey, '96 a Médoc (Cabernet Sauvignon) year, '95 excellent, '94 and '93 mixed, '92 underrated, '91 poor and '90 outstanding.

GRAPE VARIETIES

WHITES

Sauvignon Blanc Increasingly fashionable in Bordeaux. Good ones are fresh, ripe, perhaps flowery. Often blended with Sémillon.

Semillon Versatile white grape that can be intensely sweet and rich (as in Sauternes) or dryish, or off-dry (as in Graves), but with luscious notes in support. Can age very well.

REDS

Cabernet Franc Lighter, softer, thinner than Cabernet Sauvignon, and often has a slightly earthy tinge. Minor player in most blends, but important in St-Emilion and Pomerol, where it's paired with Merlot.

Cabernet Sauvignon The basis of most clarets, a grape variety with a unique and characteristic weight of fruit, held up by stout tannic walls and roofed with gutsy acidity. All these make it perfect for barrel aging and a long period of improvement in bottle. Cabernet Sauvignon, Cabernet Franc and Merlot are the three classic claret grapes.

Malbec Also known as Cot, or Pressac. A minor claret grape, though Côtes du Bourg and Premières Côtes de Blaye use it to good effect. Much more successful in Cahors (and in Argentina).

Merlot More widely grown in Bordeaux than Cabernet Sauvignon. Adds soft fruity juiciness. Merlot based wines (like St-Emilion, Pomerol) are ready to drink earlier, but many don't age so well.

Petit Verdot Difficult to ripen, but its dark, tannic, spicy flavors give quality and longevity to many fine clarets. Smells of violets.

THE PICK OF APPELLATIONS

Barsac AC Sweet white wines from a Sauternes village.

Bordeaux Blanc AC Dry white wines not designated another AC. Drink young and fresh. Some come from red wine districts where whites aren't allowed an AC.
🍷 Bordeaux Blanc de Ginestet
🍷🍷 Château Haut Mazières Blanc

Bordeaux Rosé Château de Sours is undoubtedly the best, but Château Meaume is probably the best of the rest.
🍷🍷 Château Meaume Rosé • Château Tour de Mirambeau • Château de Sours Rosé

Bordeaux Rouge AC Blanket designation for reds outside the other ACs. Variable quality.

🍷🍷 Château Haut Mazières • Château Haut Pouchard

Bordeaux Supérieur AC One up from Bordeaux Rouge, in so far as regulations go: these wines have a bit more alcohol, and yields are lower. These four reds are all of great quality for $8–$9 a bottle.

🍷 Château de Nardon

🍷🍷 Château l'Abbaye de St Fermé • Château cru Cantemerle • Château de Parenchère

Côtes de Blaye AC At their best, the reds are fresh, fruity, ready early, but at their worst cooked-tasting and tired. Some whites too.

🍷🍷 Château Grand Berthaud, Premières Côtes de Blaye

Côtes de Bourg AC At their best ripe, with full-bodied Merlot fruit and a savory edge. A good buy for St-Emilion lovers with little cash.

Côtes de Castillon AC Can produce excellent reds at low prices. Cabernet Franc and Merlot combinations.

🍷🍷 Château de Côte de Montpezat • Château Haut de la Pierrière • Seigneurs d'Aiguilhe

Côtes de Francs AC Lightish, pleasing reds for drinking fairly young. Cabernet Franc predominates. Another one to watch—quality rising sharply here.

Côtes de Fronsac (and Canon-Fronsac) AC In good

years, brilliant St-Emilion-style reds. Can be tough,
stalky and unripe otherwise.
🍷🍷 Château Mayne-Vieil
🍷🍷🍷 Château la Vieille Cure, Fronsac

Entre Deux Mers AC Traditionally bone-dry, crisp
fresh whites made from Sauvignon, often with
Sémillon.

Graves AC Good white Graves is dry yet fruity and
rounded; oak-aging lends complexity and class. Graves
Supérieur AC wines are sweeter. Also reds.
🍷🍷 Château St Jean des Graves

Haut-Médoc AC Red wine area including prestigious
names like Margaux and St Julien, but they have peeled
off into their own ACs. Wines are Cabernet Sauvignon
based and need plenty of bottle age.
🍷🍷🍷 Château d'Agassac, Cru Bourgeois • Château Magnol

Margaux AC Can be dense and chunky, but good producers and years produce spectacularly inviting reds.
Expensive.

Médoc AC Geographically the western side of the
Gironde river. The AC includes a few good, comparatively light reds for drinking young though the Cabernet Sauvignon base means they generally need bottle
age. There's more Merlot in the blend than in the Haut
Médoc.
🍷🍷🍷 Château la Cardonne, Cru Bourgeois

Monbazillac AC Sweet whites, almost Sauternes like at their best. Vineyards face north, picking up river mists that foster the botrytis or noble rot: fruit is picked over-ripe, very lightly rotted in a controlled, sweet and blowsy way.

🍷 Domaine du Haut-Rauly • Château Vignal Labrie

Pauillac AC Most famous of the Haut-Médoc communes. Latour, Lafite and Mouton-Rothschild come from here. Serious (seriously expensive) reds, austere in youth, made for aging.

🍷🍷🍷 Benjamin de Pontet Pauillac

Pessac-Léognan AC 15 year old AC from the northern part of the Graves, with typically Graves gravel soils. Sauvignon/Sémillon blends, among Bordeaux's finest—peachy, creamy at first, aging into nutty complexity. Also reds. Whites are now expensive and sought after. Few bargains here.

🍷🍷🍷 Château Haut Lagrange (red)

Pomerol AC Merlot thrives on this clay soil, and dominates Pomerol clarets, often with something delicately mineral underneath. Expensive but easy to love.

Premières Côtes de Bordeaux AC In the past, known for rather solid, workmanlike reds and sweetish whites. Quality now improving rapidly: some excellent claret bargains.

St-Emilion AC Merlot-based, the most accessible of

the "serious" clarets. Best examples are absolutely delicious, fleshy and fulsome, blackcurrant-ripe but also
minty, creamy, even raisin-tinged, perhaps with a coffee bean edge.

♟♟ Clos Magne Figeac, St-Emilion

♟♟♟ Château la Fleur Plaisance, Grand Cru • Château
Haut Bernat, St-Emilion • Château la Rose Brisson,
Grand Cru • Château Rozier, St-Emilion, Grand Cru •
Château de Dassault St-Emilion • Les Ailes de Berliquet,
St-Emilion, Grand Cru • Château Laroque St-Emilion,
Grand Cru

St Estèphe AC Least well known of the Haut-Médoc
communes, it can be a source of fine wine bargains.

♟♟♟ Château Morin, St Estèphe

St Julien AC Reds to rival those of Pauillac, and prices
too.

♟♟♟ Château du Glana, Cru Bourgeois

Sainte Croix du Mont AC Sweet whites made, like
Sauternes, from Sémillon, Sauvignon and Muscadelle.

♟♟ Château La Caussade

Sauternes AC The noble rot (botrytis) on the Semillon
grape is the mainstay of these classic pudding whites,
aided by Sauvignon Blanc and a little Muscadelle. Rich,
even viscous, but balancing lush fruit with fresh acidity.

♟♟♟ Château La Garenne Sauternes, Organic • Château Lot
Sauternes, J David (half)

BURGUNDY

This is the home of household names like Beaujolais and Chablis, as well as some of the most prized Pinot  Noirs and Chardonnays in the world. Prices are silly for good Burgundy, partly because quantities are small. The reputable wines are snapped up early, and may disappear from the retail market altogether.

The vineyard map of Burgundy is very different to that of Bordeaux. Physically, it is a different wine landscape. Bordeaux is dominated by big estates, Burgundy is a patchwork quilt of tiny properties. Bordeaux châteaux might make two or three wines; Burgundy *domaines* might make a whole range in tiny quantities, both red and white. Single varietals rule here— Chardonnay and Pinot Noir—whereas Bordeaux is about judicious blending. In Bordeaux, château-bottling has always been the norm. Here, the tradition is different: *négociants* (merchants) have acted as intermediaries, buying up fruit, and wine (blending the wines of different properties for a uniform effect), or making their own under their own labels. Things are changing in Burgundy, though, as the idea of doing their own bottling and labeling catches on with the little independent *domaines*. *Négociants* are now also beginning to buy their own vineyards.

A new generation of wine growers and makers are

shaking up the old system, and taking on New World influences. This has been controversial. The question has been asked, should Chablis really taste like Chardonnay? Shouldn't it taste more like Chablis? Should cheap Pinot Noir really be so raspberryish and simple? Shouldn't it be a bit farmyardy and challenging? Whatever the French think, as far as export markets go we are impressed that better cheap Burgundies are now beginning to appear in the stores. It's still necessary to choose very carefully, however. There's still a lot of over-priced junk wine about.

Red Burgundies can be drunk youngish, and enjoyed, but the very best *domaines*/vintages should be allowed time to mature. Cheap Bourgogne Blancs are good young and fresh, though most white Burgundy improves after four or five years. A couple of years in bottle is good even for the cheapies. Reds might need 10. The fine wine (bottles at $300, or $3000, or more) has a long, long life ahead in bottle and undergoes a magical transformation into something rich and strange if allowed to mature properly. Having said that, many wines fade by about their 15th birthday. What's fun in Burgundy is to buy the best wine you can afford, store it and try it at intervals to see how it's doing. Burgundy is full of surprises. That's how people get hooked.

"Burgundy is full of surprises. That's how people get hooked."

There are four main regions: the Côte d'Or (aka

millionaires' row) divides into the two main areas, the Côte de Beaune and the Côte de Nuits. The former is mainly white wines, the latter mainly reds. These two, the Beaune and Nuits, are the snob appellations and there are very few bargains to be had from either. The Côte Chalonnaise is looked down upon as a lesser region of lower quality but is still expensive. The Mâconnais, down in the south of the region, is regarded as a source of everyday drinking, and is cheaper. It's also a region where modern methods are turning out some delicious, not too scarily priced Chardonnay. Some. Not a lot. Beaujolais is tacked on to Burgundy though its soft juicy Gamay reds have little in common with the Côte d'Or.

The words Premier Cru in Burgundy only denote a second rank wine. Grand Cru is the top division. Remember that Grand Cru is a label awarded the land/vineyard, and NOT to the wines. Single vineyard wines attach their name to the village name.

VINTAGES

Vintages are often difficult this far north, and difficult to pronounce good or bad. They generally vary, good for one area, not so good for another. 2000 was difficult, with rain and hail at harvest. Whites are better than reds, which will be light. 1999 was pretty good, '98 patchy, '97 good for early drinking, '95 and '96 good to excellent, '94 ok-good, '93 mostly good, '92 good for whites especially; '91 was mixed, and '90 sensational. Further back, '85, '88 and '89 were also good.

GRAPE VARIETIES

WHITES

Aligoté Little seen outside Burgundy, though it appears in Eastern Europe. Can be a dull white grape, blandly rich, mundanely tart. There's some good New Wave stuff starting to emerge though.

Chardonnay Flavors and styles vary dramatically across the region. Some use oak, some not.

Pinot Beurot Local name for Pinot Gris.

Pinot Blanc Not widespread in Burgundy but used in some Côte d'Or blends and elsewhere.

REDS

Gamay Makes fresh, quaffable cherryish reds in a simple juicy style, notably the Beaujolais. All but the top wines should be drunk young.

Pinot Noir The trickiness of the Pinot Noir is what makes every red vintage here so nerve-wracking. Bad wines are dramatically bad. There's often something farmyardy and a touch vegetal in red Burgundies and bad ones can reek like a well-used stable. Good bargain wines are light and concentrated, fresh but rich, with raspberry or strawberry fruit, and a little complexity. Well-matured examples can acquire a stunning chocolate and prune richness, leathery character and layers of flavor.

THE PICK OF APPELLATIONS

Beaujolais AC The basic Beaujolais classification, covering the southern reds. Don't drink the Nouveau in November; it's meant to be drunk the following spring. Beaujolais-Villages should have more weight and depth of cherry fruit.

🍷 Olivier Ravier Beaujolais
🍷🍷 Château du Basty, Beaujolais Villages

Beaune Blanc AC Catch-all white wine Beaune appellation. Some freedom here to behave unconventionally. Louis Latour makes a high class iconoclast.
🍷🍷🍷 Beaune Blanc, Louis Latour

Bourgogne Aligoté AC A white seafood and Kir wine. Quality and fruit vary enormously. Old vine wine is occasionally exceptional. Bourgogne Aligoté de Bouzeron wines are excellent. Jayer-Gilles' delicious wine shows the potential here.
🍷🍷 Jayer-Gilles Bourgogne Aligoté

Bourgogne Blanc AC Basic white Burgundy can be horrible muck, or a great bargain. Sometimes the label is applied to "wrongly-grown" whites that have just missed out on a posher AC. The word Chardonnay is beginning to appear here.

🍷 Bourgogne Blanc Chardonnay, Buxy

🍷🍷🍷 Baron de la Charrière, Cuvée St Vincent

Bourgogne Rouge AC Basic catch-all Red Burgundy classification. There are bargains to be had from vineyards that just fail to be included in a smart AC, but not many. Much Bourgogne Rouge is still horribly rough. The words Pinot Noir are beginning to appear on labels here.

🍷🍷 Bourgogne Pinot Noir Les Piquets

Chablis AC Basic Chablis comes from a big area and encompasses the good and the gruesome. Traditionally Chablis is unoaked. New World methods are catching on and there are now fruitier, richer, more international-style Chardonnays alongside the steelier seafood wines. Much basic Chablis appears under merchants' rather than vineyard name. Co-op stuff is good—try La Chablisienne. Look out for any leftover wines from the excellent 1995/6 vintages.

🍷 Chablis Premier Cru Beauroy (half)

🍷🍷 Chablis Vau Coursières, Marguerite Carillon • Chablis, La Chablisienne

🍷🍷🍷 Chablis Vieilles Vignes, Vocoret • Chablis William Fèvre • Chablis Premier Cru, Brocard • Chablis 1er cru Les Vaillons, Vocoret

Chambertin AC Côte de Nuits AC making Grand Cru reds of world renown (and very steep prices).

Chassagne-Montrachet AC Côte de Beaune reds and whites. Everyone wants the glorious whites. The reds can be dull and crude.

Chorey-lès-Beaune AC Côtes de Beaune reds of fairly reliable quality, yet prices remain comparatively low.
🍷🍷🍷 Chorey-lès-Beaune Domaine Maillard

Côte de Beaune AC Reds and whites from the southern Côte d'Or.

Hautes Côtes de Beaune AC Hilly area making decent wine at reasonable prices. Cave des Hautes Côtes wines are a fine value.

Côte de Brouilly AC Red Beaujolais. Varies in quality.

Côte Chalonnaise AC Lean and subtle Chardonnays, though the Bourgogne Aligoté de Bouzeron is anything but. Reds from good producers can be superb, better than many Beaunes (*see* **Rully**).

Crémant de Bourgogne AC Champagne method whites and pinks, using Chardonnay and Pinot Noir. Can be good, but are often bone dry. Lots of work to do here.

Fleurie AC On a good day, an accessible, good quality, soft and lovable Beaujolais.

Gevrey-Chambertin AC Côte de Nuits reds, interna-tionally known and sought after.

Givry AC Côte Chalonnaise reds. Excellent when cher-ryish and ripe, with faintly pungent, even tarry edges.

Julienas AC Red Beaujolais: some wines prove big and serious, but the best are Fleurie-like.

Mâcon Blanc AC Traditionally lightish, subtle Chardonnays but the New Wave are making some exciting wines. Quality is hugely variable. Mâcon Blanc-Villages AC wines are judged to be from supe-rior plots to the plain Mâcon Blancs. The better ones are suffixed by a village name. The five wines listed here are all $10 and under and represent brilliant value.
🍷 Mâcon-Villages Chardonnay, Cave de Lugny
🍷🍷 Mâcon-Lugny, Louis Latour • Domaine des Deux Roches, Mâcon Davaye • Mâcon Chardonnay, Domaine les Ecuyers • Mâcon Uzichy, Raphael Sallet

Mercurey AC Half the Côte Chalonnaise's wine is in the Mercurey AC. Most of the wines are red, fruity with a touch of smoke; whites are on the way up.

Meursault AC Famous Côte de Beaune whites, though over-production has been a problem. Good ones are outstanding.

Montagny AC Côte Chalonnaise whites, traditionally

spare and dry, but growing rounder and oakier in recent years.
🍷🍷🍷 Montagny La Grande Roche, Premier Cru, Louis Latour

Monthélie AC Côtes de Beaune reds. Often overpriced but try this Oddbins New Wave wine.
🍷🍷🍷 Monthelie Rouge, Domaine du Château de Puligny-Montrachet

Puligny/Chassagne Montrachet AC Famous Côte de Beaune whites from the villages of Puligny and Chassagne. Concentrated and intense.
🍷🍷🍷 Chassagne-Montrachet, Fontaine Gagnard • Puligny-Montrachet Les Charmes, Domaine Borgeot

Morgon AC Beaujolais reds. Should acquire cocoa and rich plum flavors after bottle aging.
🍷🍷 Morgon Jean Descombes

Moulin-à-Vent AC Traditionally, big serious Beaujolais reds made for keeping, though better wines and riper years lately make them good much earlier.
🍷🍷🍷 Château des Jacques Moulin-à-Vent, Louis Jadot

Musigny AC Grand Cru Côte de Nuits reds and whites.

Nuits-St-Georges AC Côte de Nuits reds with a characteristic harmony of lightish, ripe fruit and vegetal-tinged chocolatey raisininess.

Pommard AC Côte de Beaune heavyweight reds of an old-fashioned shape and style.

Pouilly-Fuissé AC Mâconnais whites: fashionable, and can be overpriced. Look out for wines from adjoining villages, Pouilly-Loche and Pouilly-Vinzelles.
♈♈♈ Pouilly-Fuissé, Caves des Grands Cru Blancs

Régnié AC Red Beaujolais of variable quality, heavily dependent on a good summer.

La Romanée AC Sensational Côte de Nuits reds from a tiny AC. Some Viognier (peachy white grape) is allowed in with the Pinot Noir. Unbelievably expensive. If you have to ask the price . . .

Rully AC Côte Chalonnaise reds and whites which can prove to be real bargains. Whites are full and spicy thanks to the use of new oak.

St Aubin AC Côte de Beaune reds and whites, traditionally thought rustic, but improved and underrated.

St-Amour AC Beaujolais reds. Prices soar just before February 14.

St-Véran AC Mâconnais whites, long considered poor man's Pouilly-Fuissé in style, so some bargains can be had here, though lately this AC has grown complacent.
♈♈ Domaine de Curis, Louis Jadot • St-Véran Les Deux Moulins, Louis Latour

🍷🍷🍷 St-Véran Domaine des Deux Roches

Santenay AC Côte de Beaune reds, once thought rustic, improving.
🍷🍷🍷 Santenay-Gravières Premier Cru, Roger Belland

Sauvignon de St-Bris Sauvignon Blanc is not permitted in this precise spot so an AC was denied. Not always as good as its hype, but can be very decent, fruity and fresh.

Savigny-lès-Beaune AC One or two good whites coming out of this AC.

LOIRE

There are signs of change in the traditionalist Loire. More domaine-bottled wine is appearing, as wine-growers realize they can also be winemakers, and don't have to sell their fruit on to the co-op. There is recognition here that the world craves more individual wines, not great lakes of drinkable but mediocre stuff. There is change in wine-making methods too.

This far north, it's difficult to ripen fruit properly. Sauvignon Blanc, a grape which likes cool conditions as long as it sees some sun, is well suited to the Loire climate. This was the premier Sauvignon specialist region of the world until New Zealand arrived on the

"... traditional, flinty, subtle wines have been joined by rich, fruity New Wave bottles that have the critics divided."

scene, prompting a thousand New World imitators. Oak was never, traditionally, a Loire. Sauvignon freshness and acidity would have been drowned out by woody dryness. But now, barrel-use is creeping in, both for fermentation and for oak-aging. New World methods are making a big impact here: macerating wines on their skins, to extract as much grape color and flavor as possible, is now commonplace. In effect, there are now two Loires, old and new; this is seen perhaps most vividly in Sancerre, where traditional, flinty, subtle wines have been joined by rich, fruity New Wave bottles that have the critics divided. The situation is very similar to that of Burgundy. Alain Gueneau is typical of the New Wave here. He has a small property, very high standards, oversees the growing and making of wine, and takes a modern, hi-tech approach. The result is the deliciously unconventional Sancerre Blanc La Guiberte.

One thing is clear—the New World approach here, in squeezing every last drop of color and flavor out of the fruit, should make Loire red a much more viable, loveable prospect, and also, crucially, make the Loire much less vintage-dependent.

The Loire divides into three regions. The western Loire is dominated by Muscadet. The central Loire is the Chenin Blanc belt (sweet botrytised Chenins can be superb), where they also grow Cabernet Franc reds (Chinon), and some Sauvignon Blanc under the Touraine AC. The upper Loire is the Sauvignon belt proper, home of Sancerre and Menetou-Salon, as well as Pinot Noir reds.

The last edition of the guide said that Muscadet is rarely worth the effort of getting the cork out of the bottle. The Melon de Bourgogne grape is basically an inferior, dull variety which should be grubbed up and replaced with more interesting vines. If this were the New World it would have happened long ago, but the French have a strong sense of tradition and would be totally scandalized by the very idea. A huge amount of effort is going into improving Muscadet and though there's still far too much pointless, dreary wine about, there are also a few good ones emerging which show the potential here. Only buy the wine made Sur Lie (on the lees), meaning the wine has been allowed to remain on its yeasty base, unfiltered, for a time to gain creamy complexity and a semi-spritzy texture. Non Sur Lie bottles are rarely worth buying.

VINTAGES

It's difficult to generalize, as a cold summer might produce gorgeous Sauvignon Blancs, tart unripe Chenins and tough green reds. The 2000 vintage was beset by storms, rain and hail but looks like a good year. Wines are rich but with good acidity. 1999 was mixed, fair to excellent; 1998 not very good (other than for sweet Chenins), though '95, '96 and '97 were excellent. 1997's warm summer was better for reds than whites. 1996 was a particularly good sweet wine year. 1990 and '93 were good all round. 1992 and '94 were better for whites than reds.

GRAPE VARIETIES

WHITES

Chardonnay More commonly grown in the Loire than it used to be. Generally pared down, lean and tangy. Less good specimens taste thin and unripe.

Chenin Blanc This grape variety drinks up sun; less competently grown/made or weather-blighted Chenins are lean and over-subtle. Moist, warm conditions are ideal for sweet (botrytised) Chenins.

Melon de Bourgogne The Muscadet grape.

Sauvignon Blanc The Pouilly-Fumé and Sancerre grape, and the basis of Sauvignon de Touraine.

REDS

Cabernet Franc The quality red grape of Anjou and Touraine. Depending on vineyard, intentions and the weather, wines range from light and simple gluggers to big, serious wines made for aging.

Cabernet Sauvignon Tricky in these northern climes. Frequently used to lend substance to red blends.

Gamay Hit and miss quality for the Beaujolais grape up this far north. Bad ones can be unripe, harsh and thin.

Pinot Noir Similar problems to Gamay. Even the cherryish and aromatic good ones are pretty insubstantial.

THE PICK OF APPELLATIONS

Anjou AC Whites can be green and insubstantial, the reds light at best, the Gamays vegetal, and the pinks, using the mediocre Grollean grape variety, sweet and insipid. Cabernet d'Anjou pinks are usually better. Anjou-Villages is the red AC to look out for.
🍷 Domaine des Hardiers Anjou-Villages

Bourgueil AC Increasingly fashionable Touraine reds, often tough and disappointing when young, but acquiring fruit, depth and class with bottle age.
🍷 Les Chevaliers Bourgueil

Chinon AC A bit of a cult red. Good Chinon from warm, ripe years is delicious; otherwise, acids and tannins can overwhelm the fruit.
🍷 Chinon Domaine de Briancon • Chinon Domaine de Colombier
🍷🍷 Château de Coulaine • Chinon-lès-Garous, Couly-Dutheil • Les Petits Roches, Chinon Charles Joguet

Coteaux du Giennois AC Northerly little-known Loire appellation beginning to attract attention.

Coteaux du Layon AC Delicious sweet whites, traditionally laid down for ten or 20 years to acquire a honeyed richness. Sélections de Grains Nobles (botrytised) are the sweetest.
🍷🍷 Domaine du Plessis • Château de la Genaiserie • Coteaux du Layon Chaume

Crémant de Loire AC Sparkling wines, usually kinder and more lovable than Saumur.
🍷🍷 Langlois Crémant de Loire

Menetou-Salon AC Reds and roses are average quality, but the whites can rival Sancerre on a good day. Henry Pellé is the man.
🍷🍷 Menetou-Salon, Domaine Henry Pellé • Menetou-Salon Domaine Fournier

Muscadet de Sèvre-et-Maine AC The only Muscadet worth drinking. Good ones have a round, creamy character, fresh lemony edge, and a semi-spritzy texture from being left Sur Lie (on the lees). Some are tangy and fruity, others mineral and salty.

🍷 Muscadet Sur Lie, Château la Touche • Muscadet Sur Lie, Côtes de Grandlieu, Guerin • Muscadet Sur Lie, Domaine de Vieux Chai

Pouilly-Fumé AC Across the river from Sancerre. Supposedly, Pouilly-Fumés are fruitier and rounder, but in practice it's difficult to tell the difference. They should also be mineral-edged and elegant. Some have faintly gooseberryish fruit and a hyacinth-floral edge. You will pay $12+ for a good one.

🍷🍷 Pouilly-Fumé Les Adelins • Pouilly-Fumé Chatelain • Pouilly-Fumé Domaine des Rabichattes • Pouilly-Fumé Masson-Blondelet

Quincy AC Competent, though rarely outstanding Sauvignon Blancs.

🍷🍷 Quincy, Clos des Victoires

Reuilly AC Sauvignon Blanc bargains can occasionally be found here, from this upper Loire appellation close to Sancerre.

🍷🍷 Reuilly, Henri Beurdin

Sancerre AC Drink these Sauvignons young to best enjoy those fruity, goosegog and nettle flavors. Some are too subtle, though, nutty and green but under-

fruited and thin. These can seem severely overvalued at
$12+. There's also a Sancerre Rouge AC, making Pinot
Noirs.

♟♟ Sancerre Chavignol, Paul Thomas • Sancerre Domaine
Naudet • Sancerre La Guiberte, Alain Gagneau • Sancerre
Domaine Fournier Vieilles Vignes
♟♟♟ Sancerre Domaine Vacheron

Saumur AC Champagne-method sparkling Chenins
(or Chenin blends), usually flabby and mediocre. The
best have dry apple fruit.

♟♟ Saumur 96, Château de Montgueret

Saumur Blanc AC Usually very dry Chenin, but some
are sweeties.

♟♟ Saumur Blanc Vieilles Vignes, Domaine Langlois

Saumur-Champigny AC Reliable Cabernet-based
reds. Vieilles Vignes are best.

♟♟ Château de Targe, Saumur-Champigny

Touraine AC Really good Sauvignon de Touraine rivals
Sancerre for flavor and quality, but at half the price.
There has been steep improvement in this AC in the
last four years. Joel Delaunay is a good Touraine
name. Reds are less dependable, though Gamays are
improving.

♟ Waitrose Touraine • Sauvignon de Touraine Joel
Delaunay • Sauvignon de Touraine Maison Brulées

Vin de Pays du Jardin de la France Dull whites; occasional good ones are fruity and tangy. Cheap and cheerful. Usually just cheap.

Vouvray AC Chenin Blanc Vouvray's been in the doldrums but is on the up again. Good ones have fruit and poise even in youth, but also age well, acquiring delectable creamy fruity honeyed flavors. Choose from sec (dry) and demi-sec (off-dry): in reality, styles range from medium-dryish to full and fruity. The very sweet dessert wine—Moelleux—can be one of the world's most exciting dessert wines, but needs bottle age.

🍷 Vouvray, Domaine Pouvraie

🍷🍷 Vouvray Gaston d'Orléans • Vouvray Les Chaires Salées • Vouvray Les Garadières • Vouvray Demi-Sec Domaine Bourillon d'Orléans

🍷🍷🍷 Vouvray Tris des Grains Nobles, Bourillon d'Orléans

RHÔNE

Despite its cluster of star appellations and world renown among the collectors, the Rhône continues to be undervalued and neglected by many wine hunters. It's seen as old-fashioned. Bordeaux is classy, Burgundy sexy, and the Rhône? The Rhône is rustic. But this is unfair. Not only does the northern Rhône have some of the world's most sought after red wine, but there are also real bargains to be had. At the $8–$12 level the Rhône

has a lot to offer, though not usually in its famous ACs.
Good cheap Rhône has a lot going for it—rich fruit, a
subtle earthiness, lots of individuality. Some of it is
rustic, but in an appealing way. It's good with food.
Other reds (and it is reds we're talking about, though
some good white is also made) are surprisingly elegant, complex, delicious. This is a region that repays a
little exploration. It still can't compare with Languedoc
for stunning fruit for $8–$10, but it's getting there. Or
rather it could get there, if it could only get its act
together.

The Rhône falls into northern and southern camps.
Most wine is made in the south, where the hills give
way to the plain. In the north, where craggy hillside
vineyards grow tiny quantities of fruit, Syrah dominates. Big gutsy reds are made here, the world-class
reds collectors crave. Côte-Rôtie is the snobbiest AC.
There are also star names like Crozes-Hermitage,
Hermitage itself, and the Viognier grape favorite, Condrieu. In the south, where Grenache dominates (usually in Grenache Syrah blends) and where hillsides give
way to a hot river plain, things are patchier, with big
names like Châteauneuf-du-Pape generally failing to
live up to their reputations, but straight Côtes du
Rhône and Côtes du Rhône Villages are improving
fast, along with other, less well known southern ACs.
Lots of medium-weight country red comes out of
here, alongside richer, more interesting bargains. The
potential is huge—the New World has shown what can
be done with Syrah(Shiraz)-Grenache; the demand for
these rich fruity, savory-spicy blends is enormous. The

Rhône could deliver, with a little imagination and an overhaul of technique.

It is beginning to happen, but it's early days. There are still problems. The main one is the greedily high vineyard yields and plain incompetence in the wine-making that follows. Many potentially good reds are still being ruined by spending too long in old (far too old) oak, when early bottling would have made the most of their fruity, spicy, peppery Rhône character.

Rhône whites can be interesting. This is the home of Viognier, now, like Shiraz and Grenache, so huge in the New World. Marsanne and Roussanne, currently very big in Australia, are also Rhône natives. Usually they are used in blends. There is so much potential here, if the Rhône would only take on Australia's expertise in making these often-dull grapes sing out with fruit and sun and personality.

VINTAGES

2000 was another good year in a trio of impressive vintages—'98 and '99 were also good, and are very good values. 1997 was patchy, '96 pretty good in the north, patchy in the south; 1995 fantastic, '94 and '93 pretty poor. 1992 was okay, '91 good for the north, and '90 brilliant all around.

GRAPE VARIETIES

WHITES

Clairette Used solo in some of the big, beefy (dreary) whites of the south; better when teamed with Muscat in Crémant/Clairette de Die.

Grenache Blanc Much seen in the southern Rhône. Subtle, pear-fruited with spice on the finish. Good in the right hands.

Marsanne The main white Crozes-Hermitage grape. A tricky variety: bad ones are just big and dull, but good 'uns are fruity, rich, buttery.

Muscat Best known in the rich and voluptuous sweetie, Muscat de Beaumes de Venise. Also used with Clairette in Rhône sparklers.

Roussanne Light and aromatic whites in both north and south. Star names attract high prices.

Ugni Blanc Mediocre cheap white grape of the south. Padding for blends.

Viognier Now hugely popular thanks to a revival sparked in the New World. Dry and sweet versions are made of this rich, peachy, alcoholic, musky, gently spiced, perhaps slightly viscous white. Condrieu, the original Rhône Viognier star, commands high prices but often disappoints.

REDS

Carignan Janus-faced, responsible for mediocre cheapo reds and old vine Carignan, wines that are rich, fruity, full of depth and quality.

Cinsaut Useful in blends and much used in pinks, to which it adds spice and freshness.

Counoise Spicy red best known for its work in Châteauneuf-du-Pape.

Grenache The workhorse red grape of the south, at once light and fruity, with a twist of pepper and spice.

Mourvèdre A big, often tannic red popular in blends, but used solo in Bandol down in Provence, where it shows its capacity to age.

Syrah Main red grape of northern Rhône, explosively tannic, concentrated and raw in youth, but soft, fruity, blackcurranty, plummy when mature.

THE PICK OF APPELLATIONS

Châteauneuf-du-Pape AC Good reds are deeply, richly fruity, almost sweet, gently but firmly structured. Or they can be a dark and impenetrable soup of fruit pastille. In a bad summer, raw and harsh. Thirteen different grapes are allowed. Whites also made. Few bargains here and lots of overrated, complacent red.
🍷🍷🍷 Châteauneuf-du-Pape, Domaine de la Solitude • Châteauneuf-du-Pape, Domaine Font de Michelle • Châteauneuf-du-Pape, Michel Bernard • Perrin Châteauneuf-du-Pape, Les Sinards

Condrieu AC Famous Viognier from the north. Rich, apricot-edged nectar, or dull and over-rated. It depends on which bottle you buy. Certainly expensive.
🍷🍷🍷 Condrieu Les Chaillets, Yves Cuilleron • Condrieu, Marcel Guigal

Cornas AC Northern Rhône reds of big, beefy, rustic style.

Costières de Nîmes AC Always good value, but now beginning to show star quality. This AC straddles Rhône and Languedoc and tastes like it. New Wave Rhônes! Syrah Grenache blends with raspberries and spice, like Château Guiot. Immensely reliable; stock up for parties.
🍷 Plan Macassan • Château Guiot • Château Lamargue • Château de Nages

🍷🍷 Château de Valcombe • Château de Surville

Coteaux du Tricastin AC Good, simple southern Rhône reds (and okay whites).
🍷 Domaine de Grangeneuve

Côte-Rotie AC Drop dead trendy northern Rhône reds, sometimes even worth the hype. Oddly, a little Viognier, a peachy white, is added to the red. Odder still, Syrah-Viognier blends have not yet emerged from Australia. Mega-expensive.

Côtes du Lubéron AC Generally light-bodied, pleasant peasant glug from the south. Reds and some whites.

Côtes du Rhône AC Good reds are really fresh, full of fruit, made for drinking young (though others turn up big and black, full of tannin, obviously with different intentions). There are also whites.
🍷 Caveau des Disciples • Enclave des Papes Cuvée Special
• La Chasse du Pape
🍷🍷 Clos Petite Bellane • Côtes du Rhône Mule Noire • Côtes du Rhône, Guigal

Côtes du Rhône Blanc AC Clos Petite Bellane is a 50/50 Viognier/Roussanne blend, full-bodied with sweet fruit and a dry, waxy, nutty quality typical of Rhône whites.

🍷🍷 Clos Petite Bellane Côtes du Rhône Blanc • Côtes du Rhône Chaume Arnaud

Côtes du Rhône Villages AC 17 villages can add their name to the label, e.g. Rasteau. Good reds have fresh raspberry, perhaps a little porty alcohol, an earthy note and spice. Whites are improving.

🍷 Tesco Finest Côtes du Rhône Villages Reserve, Domaine de la Grand Retour • Rasteau Côtes du Rhône Villages Tesco 5

🍷🍷 Beaumes de Venise, Terroir de Trias • Château Trignon, Sablet Ramillades • Domaine de l'Arneillaud Cairanne

Côtes du Ventoux AC Southern Rhône reds (plus some pinks and whites), usually sound, simple, good value, but occasionally pull rabbits out of hats.

🍷 La Tour du Prévot

Crozes-Hermitage AC Can fall into the easy-going and juicy camp, but the best offer a glimpse of greatness, with structure, smoke and spice on top of good solid fruit. The whites are (usually) less impressive and everything is too pricey. It's difficult to find decent wine under $15.

🍷🍷 Crozes-Hermitage, Domaine du Pavilion Mercuriol

Gigondas AC Grenache-based southern reds which

straddle the frontier between fine wine and rustic glug. Prices are rising.

⚑⚑ Gigondas Domaine Paillère et Pied

⚑⚑⚑ Gigondas Château de Trignon • Gigondas Guigal

Hermitage AC The reds are famed for their great capacity to age. No bargains. $45 is a fairly routine price here.

Muscat de Beaumes de Venise AC Southern fortified whites from the only Muscat-growing village in the Rhône. Golden, rich, viscous but also fresh and grapey dessert wines.

Vacqueyras AC Reds can be excellent, pinks okay, whites more hit and miss.

⚑⚑ Domaine de la Soleiade • Vacqueyras Perrin • Vacqueyras Beaumes de Venise

Vin de Pays Rhône Vin de Pays reds are improving, taking inspiration from their Languedoc neighbor.

⚑ Vin de Pays des Bouches du Rhône: Domaine de l'Île St Pierre, Cabernet Franc

⚑⚑ Vin de Pays du Gard: Mas de Guiot Cabernet Syrah

THE SOUTH

It's Vin de Pays that best challenges the New World in France, and the south is the heartland of the Vin de Pays revival. The really interesting area is the Languedoc: look for Vin de Pays d'Oc and Coteaux du

Languedoc bottles which can produce excellent wines (mostly reds) at bargain prices. Other southern areas are also improving fast: Corbières and Minervois, also Languedoc appellations, are on the turn. Dull old Fitou is also beginning to turn up some excellent wines. Côtes du Roussillon—farther down the south-west corner, knocking at Spain's border—is starting to show New Wave influence too. Areas straddling the Languedoc and Rhône, notably Costières de Nîmes, are producing superb reds. This whole swathe of land, most of it contained within the traditional regional borders of the Midi, is transforming itself from the vast lake of so-so wine into a source not only of delicious

> "The often baked-tasting, flabby, dirty, rustic reds and sad sludgy whites of the old days are disappearing…"

country wines, but also classy numbers that taste three times their price. The Languedoc especially is developing its own star appellations with wines that have knocked the socks off visiting critics, like the immensely influential Robert Parker from the U.S. Mas de Daumas Gassac has become a celebrity domaine with its extraordinary Bordeaux-taste-alikes that have left the claret producers further north spluttering with rage and envy. It has been suggested (by Bordeaux) that Merlot, Cabernet Sauvignon and Cabernet Franc should be prohibited grapes down here in France's New World. They should stick to their traditional red blends, involving Carignan, Syrah,

Grenache, Mourvèdre and Cinsaut. The best of these blends have rich fruit but also keep a really local feel about them, perhaps with subtle flavors of the garrigue, an arid, rocky landscape of wild thyme and rosemary, laurel and lavender.

New World winemaking techniques are key to the turnaround. Australians, New Zealanders, and other outsiders have been key catalysts. The all too often baked-tasting, flabby, dirty, rustic reds and sad sludgy whites of the old days are disappearing and delicious, precise, fruity, elegant wines taking their place. Some of the results are better and more original than the New World can make at the price. Some wineries are actually owned by outsiders. Australian giant BRL Hardys owns La Baume. Penfolds has now bought out James Herrick. Australians are also behind the excellent Abbots label. Other investors are moving in.

New Wave influence has led to the mass planting of Chardonnay. There's an awful lot of Chardonnay Vin de Pays d'Oc about, not all of it good. Plenty of single varietal Sauvignon, Viognier, Cabernet Sauvignon and Merlot is also popping up because that's what the locals have been told the world is after. The answer to this is yes and no. As far as cheap, sub $8 inferior quaffers are concerned, yes. The world can't get enough of it. But times are changing and palates becoming more sophisticated. The traditional red and white blends of this region have a huge future if they can concentrate on applying New World methods but retaining local character.

GRAPE VARIETIES

The southwest closest to Bordeaux shows that influence with lots of bargain "claret" wines, Merlot and Cabernet Sauvignon-based wines. Bordeaux style whites are made too, with Sauvignon and Semillon, plus some Muscadelle for sweet wines like Monbazillac. Ugni Blanc and Colombard make sharp, tangy whites in Gascony.

Go east into the Lot and you find Cahors, the big Malbec (Auxerrois) zone, with some Merlot. Further east it gets more varied: the great vineyard plains of mid and eastern Languedoc show Rhône influences with lots of Syrah and Grenache, plus Mourvèdre (and Cinsaut and Counoise). Carignan begins to loosen its grip. Whites get more quirky; local Picpoul de Pinet makes fragrant soft whites, fruity but with good freshness (Picpoul could be a New World star?). Chenin works well with Grenache Blanc and Chardonnay. Sauvignon and Sémillon, like Merlot and Cabernet Sauvignon, need a maritime climate and don't work inland.

In the southwest of Languedoc, Carignan dominates, with the aid of Cinsaut, Grenache, Syrah and Mourvèdre. Syrah is becoming more important. Corbières and Fitou grow lots of Carignan on the plains, plus Grenache. Syrah grows on the Corbières hillsides; Mourvèdre by the sea. Further south towards the Pyrenees, some truly local grapes take over. Sturdy, rustic Tannat rules the reds. The white Mauzac grape is a bulk and fizz favorite. Petit Manseng is the white grape of sweet Jurançon; Pacherenc de Vic Bilh uses Gros and Petit Manseng, and Arufiat. These aren't grapes that pop up anywhere else.

Roussillon has a vin doux naturel tradition. Maury and Banyuls are sweet red wines, Grenache-based, the closest thing France has to port. The muscats, notably Muscat de Rivesaltes, are more famous. Some are honey gold and grapey, others dark from oxidation. The Hérault also has vin doux naturel: Muscats de Lunel, Frontignan and Mireval.

VINTAGES

1999 was a great year throughout the South of France. 1997 was hit and miss, but '98 was superb—drink them up! 2000 was stormy and patchy but in general of good quality thanks to improved technique.

THE PICK OF APPELLATIONS

Bergerac AC Merlot-based claret-type reds; often rustic, but at their best offering faint echoes of St-Emilion. Côtes de Bergerac reds are more alcoholic.

Bergerac Sec AC The Bergerac whites, dullish with the exception of the excellent Sauvignon-dominated La Jaubertie wines. Côtes de Bergerac wines are sweeter.

Bandol AC In Provence. Mourvèdre-based big reds which age well, spicy pinks, plus decent good Rhône-style whites. Provence's top AC, beloved of a million tourists, and prices reflect this.

Banyuls AC Vin Doux Naturel Grenache sweet reds; some dryish.

Buzet AC Another claret-style AC from a Bordeaux neighbor. Some are good but too many are raw, tannic and sappy-green.

Cabardes AC North Western Languedoc appellation not far from Carcassonne. On the way up. Delicious rustic reds.
🍷 Château Depaule Cabardes
🍷🍷 Abbots Cirrus

Cahors AC Big, hearty, pruney Malbec-based reds, some with Merlot and Tannat, traditionally the "Black Wines" used to boost lean Bordeaux vintages. Lighter, juicier Cahors is also made.

Collioure AC Grenache-based, sturdy reds from close to the Spanish border. Château de Jau wines are reliable.

Corbières AC One of those turnaround Languedoc ACs: old-fashioned rustic bottles nestle by New Wave bargains on the shelves. Some New Wave reds are just too light and lean but good Corbières combines rich dark fruit with herbs and something flinty.
🍷 Corbières Reserve, La Sansoure • Château Haut St George Corbières • Château des Lanes Corbières

🍷🍷 Christiane Limouzi Corbières • Château St Auriol •
Domaine de Villemajou • Château de Caraguilhes • Château
Ollieux Romanis

Costières du Nîmes AC *see* **Rhône**

Coteaux d'Aix en Provence AC Decent reds and pinks
from an improving AC.

Coteaux du Languedoc AC Mostly reds. Large
umbrella AC consisting of 12 little ones, like Pic St
Loup. Wines vary, but this is the outstanding Languedoc AC. From $6 reds like Le Maquis, to emerging
stars like Château l'Hospitalet at the rather unfortunately named La Clape (it's the name of a local hill,
just south of Narbonne) this is a little country unto
itself and repays exploration, with or without compass.
🍷 Le Maquis • Château Valoussière • Mas St Vincent
🍷🍷 Ermitage du Pic St Loup • Château Boisset, La Clape •
Château Flauguergues • Château l'Hospitalet Summum, La
Clape • Château Pech Redon, La Clape • Château l'Euzière,
Pic St Loup • Domaine Clavel Copa Santa
🍷🍷🍷 Les Flacons Picpoul de Pinet (white) • Château
l'Hospitalet, Cuvée Beatrice, La Clape

Côtes de Duras AC Bordeaux satellite. Claret-graped,
fruity (if sometimes stalky) reds and Sauvignon-Sémil-
lon whites. Better whites are pure Sauvignon.

Côtes du Frontonnais AC Another from the Bordeaux
side. Claret-graped, or perhaps rustic peppery reds and

pinks. Negrette, a Malbec relation, is traditional; Cabernet Franc getting more common.

Côtes de Provence AC Lots of cheap quaffing wine for tourists, most of it rosé. Also big serious reds like this brooding organic Syrah.
🍷🍷🍷 Côtes de Provence Domaine Richeaume Organic Syrah

Côtes du Roussillon AC Côtes du Roussillon Villages reds are the best here. Rousillon reds can be rough and ready, rustic and warming, herby and delicious. Bad ones are overbaked by that blistering southern sun and not too cleanly made. Some classy bottles are starting to emerge now, following in Languedoc's lead.

🍷🍷 Domaine Lafage, Cuvée Lea • Château Planezes, Côtes du Roussillon Villages

Faugères AC Serious Languedoc reds, Grenache and Syrah based, with Mourvèdre and Carignan. Big beefy fruit with gamey/pruney edges. Stern pinks also.
🍷 Château de Laurens
🍷🍷 Moulin de Ciffre

Fitou AC Like Corbières, its neighbor, Fitou reds can be old-fashioned, rustic and rough-edged, but the New Wave is delivering more fruit and shape. It's also delivering big profits: good Corbières can now cost $13 a

bottle. Mostly they're Carignan-based, though some are Syrah. Fitou les Douzes ($9) is bold and brambly with a touch of savory mulberry.
🍷🍷 Fitou les Douzes, Mont Tauch • Fitou Terroirs de Tuchan

Jurançon AC Whites: some florally dry, some desserty but fresh.

Limoux AC Chardonnay-based whites are improving here. Best known for its fizz (Blanquette or Crémant) which are traditionally Mauzac-based, though that savory dryness is giving way to clean modern Chardonnay/Chenin blends. Bargains here.

Madiran AC Red country wines, can be good, though the Tannat base can make them overly rustic, tannic and chunky.

Maury AC Slightly odd but comforting sweet reds.
♟ Maury Les Vignerons du Val d'Orbieu

Minervois AC Big activity here, big change in this Corbières neighbor. Traditionally reds were fairly light and peppery, although the weightier, fruitier style the New World introduced has been hugely influential. Look out for La Livinière on labels—a quality Minervois sub-region. St Jean de Minervois muscat sweeties make superb aperitif and dessert whites.
♟ Minervois Alain Grignon
♟♟ Abbots Cumulus Minervois • Château Maris, Comte Cathare • Abbaye de

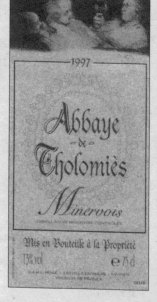

1997

Abbaye
– de –
Tholomiès

Minervois

APPELLATION MINERVOIS CONTROLÉE

Mis en Bouteille à la Propriété
13% vol   e 75 cl

Tholomies Minervois • Domaine
Borie de Maurel, Spirit
d'Automne • Domaine
de Blayac Minervois •
Le Grand Verdier •
Minervois La
Livinière, Domaine
des Aire Hautes •
Château de Landure
Minervois • Domaine Borie
de Maurel, La Feline

Montpeyroux AC Languedoc reds and whites of
decent to excellent quality. Spend $11+ for a good one.
🍷🍷 Domaine Coste Blanque • Domaine l'Aigueliere Grenat,
Montpeyroux

Muscat de Rivesaltes AC Delectable Roussillon dessert wines.

Pacharenc du Vic-Bilh AC Delicate oily whites, perhaps pear and apple-scented. Sweet Moelleux versions are also made.

Pécharmant AC Bergerac reds aged for at least 12 months before release. Can be good, with fruity depth and claret-like complexity.

St Chinian AC Some seriously good Languedoc reds, though that seriousness means young ones can be closed-up and stalky like a young Bordeaux. Divides into two main types depending on vineyard site: schist-grown ones are lighter; clay-grown wines are richer and can age. Old vineyard (vieilles vignes) wines are popular for their rich dark fruit. Spend $9–$12.
🍷🍷 Château Cazal Cuvée des Fées, Vieilles Vignes • Château de Combebelle • Domaine de Tudery St Chinian, Vieilles Vignes

Château de Combebelle

Saint-Chinian
Appellation Saint-Chinian Contrôlée

1998

TRADITION
COMTE CATHARE

MIS EN BOUTEILLE AU CHATEAU
PAR SURL COMBEBELLE 34360 VILLESPASSANS - FRANCE
13% vol.   PRODUCT OF FRANCE   750 ml

St Jean de Minervois AC *see* **Minervois**. This fortified Muscat is delicious ($9 a half).

🍷🍷 Domaine de Montahuc Muscat Comte Cathare

Vin de Pays des Côtes de Gascogne Up in Gascony, between Bordeaux and the Midi, and its wines taste like neither. Traditionally an area for Armagnac; Armagnac's Ugni Blanc and Colombard grapes are also used for fresh, sharp country whites. Sauvignon and Chardonnay too. Good for budget summer quaffers.

🍷 Domaine Le Puts, Michel Bordes • Domaine de Joy

Vin de Pays de l'Aude Up and coming for cheap cheerful wines, good for an afternoon in the hammock. All these are $6 and under. The Cuvée de Richard Blanc is actually a vin de table Francais, having failed to qualify even for Vin de Pays de l'Aude status. But it's excellent—cheapie white of the year, possibly, at around $4.50.

🍷 Devereux Portan Carignan • Domaine de Richard • Cuvée de Richard Blanc

VIN DE PAYS D'OC

In wine terms, a gigantic region. Quality has never been better, or wines more various, though there are still plenty of stinkers out there. Single varietals have become the norm here, following the New World model, and so wines are listed by grape variety.

> "Quality has never been better ... though there are still plenty of stinkers out there."

The Languedoc, shortened to d'Oc in its Vin de Pays title, has discovered it can make single varietals and varietal combinations traditional elsewhere in a rich fruity style at low prices: in other words, the Languedoc has become a New World country. It also has masses of old vines, long undervalued and used for bulk wine, but now coming into their own, producing rich deliciously fruity wine from these mature old vineyards.

There's plenty of ordinary, bland, international style wine. But there are also Loire-style Sauvignons, New Zealand-style Sauvignons, Grenache-Syrah Rhône reds, Burgundy-like or Australian-style Chardonnays, New World-style Viognier and Marsanne, and Claret blend reds that outdo Bordeaux.

WHITES

Chardonnay

♟ Domaine Raissac Chardonnay • Laperouse Chardonnay • James Herrick Chardonnay
♟♟ Borie de Maurel Chardonnay • Laroche Grand Cuvée Chardonnay • Les Grands Rochers Chardonnay • Domaine de Bousquet Chardonnay
♟♟♟ F Chardonnay

Marsanne
🍷 Le Fauve Marsanne

Sauvignon Blanc
🍷 Tesco Simply Sauvignon • Fortant de France Sauvignon Blanc • Réserve St Marc Sauvignon Blanc

Viognier
🍷 Les Fontanelles Viognier Foncalieu • Domaine du Bois Viognier, Vedeau • Domaine du Cazel Viel Viognier • La Baume Viognier
🍷🍷 Domaine de Ciffre Viognier • Domaine Complazens Blanc

Other Whites
🍷 La Source Chardonnay Roussanne • Picpoul de Pinet Château Petit Roubie • Les Grandes Vignes Chardonnay Viognier

REDS

Cabernet Sauvignon
🍷 Domaine Remaury Cabernet Sauvignon • Domaine Vistoule Cabernet Sauvignon

Merlot
🍷 Domaine de Contenson Merlot

Syrah
🍷 Domaine de Rodes Syrah

🍷🍷 James Herrick Millia Passum Syrah

Red Blends
🍷 Cuvée Simone, James Herrick
🍷🍷 Domaine Montlobre • Jean Louis Denois Mourvèdre Grenache • La Cuvée Mythique • L'Ermitage, Domaine Camplazens • Mas des Bressades Cabernet Syrah

CAMPLAZENS L'ERMITAGE
VIN DE PAYS D'OC
ÉLEVÉ • EN • FÛTS
DE CHÊNE
MCMCVIII
1998

GERMANY

In Britain they tend to look down on German wine, which is surprising considering they are Germany's most important market, taking almost 50% of their wine exports. The suspicion is easy to understand, though. It can be squarely placed at the doors of the producers of dreadful sugar-water styles like Liebfraumilch, Piesporter Michelsberg and 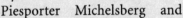 Bereich Niersteiner. Because of all the Blue Nun damage that has been inflicted on Britain and the U.S., German wines are vastly underestimated and ignored in droves. Yet German wines, in particular German Rieslings, are among the finest and most delicious in the world. Ask any wine critic to name their desert-island, dream-wine case, and a German Riesling would feature, for sure.

German wine can take a little getting used to. First you must set aside the tyrannical big lemony fruit, cream and sweet oak white wine model created by New World Chardonnay. Fine German wine is extraordinarily poised, with seamless fruit and acid complexity. Every Riesling tastes a little different to the next, some extraordinarily so. No whites are more polished and elegant. Lowish alcohol levels (often right down at 9%) let natural fruit and mineral flavors shine through.

For the quality on offer, German prices are low. $8 bottles of fine 10-year-old Mosel are not something you'll find an equivalent for anywhere else. Wine shops are littered with 1992s, '93s, '94s at ridiculously low prices. Spend $12 (the price of a bog standard Reserve Chardonnay from South Australia) and you are in the super-league, tasting wines of breathtaking complexity and finesse. Top of the range small-parcel stuff, at $18–$24 a bottle, is still priced at mere pennies when compared to equivalent quality in Burgundy or Bordeaux.

Tafelwein Table wine, usually dosed up with sugar. Occasionally, good varietal wine from a good producer, made outside the rules will be labeled thus. Concerned that you won't be able to tell the difference between the duff and the designer tafelwein? Worry not. The price will tell you all you need to know.

Landwein Country Wine, supposedly the Vin de Pays of Germany. Regions of origin are specified. Less sugar is permitted than in tafelwein.

QbA The lowest reliable quality mark. The literal translation is "decent stuff from an official region" (Qualitätswein bestimmter Anbaugebiete). That Region, the grape variety and a dry/sweetness indicator like *halbtrocken* might be all that's mentioned. A vineyard name can be listed if at least 85% of the fruit is from one source. In general, stick with QmP.

QmP Qualitätswein mit Prädikat, or in English, top quality. No sugar allowed. QmP wines are the ones that show a ripeness classification: Kabinett, Spätlese, Auslese, Beerenauslese or Trockenbeerenauslese, in ascending order from dry to very sweet.

Most fine wine for everyday drinking is Kabinett or Spätlese. Ausleses are not always straightforwardly sweet, but are often rich and faintly desserty. Beerenausleses are dense and honeyed, and are usually made from grapes affected by botrytis, or noble rot. Good Beerenauslese is associated with the Riesling grape but can also be superb when made from Scheurebe, or Silvaner. Trockenbeerenauslese is made by hand selecting individual nobly rotted grapes, which accounts for the incredible sweetness, and also the price.

At the other end of the scale, *trocken* means dry; it can mean very dry and unripe in a cool summer, especially if not from the Pfalz. *Halbtrocken* means off-dry, or medium dry. *Trocken* wines from Mosel in particular can be extremely green, and grapefruit-pith dry in the mouth. Pfalz dry wines are often the most successful, though there are many duffers even from here.

Wherever it comes from, *Trocken* is a risky choice. Better to go for a (non-*Trocken*) Kabinett—this is the choice to make for everyday drinking. Or even Spätlese: there may be sweetness in there, but it is undercut by piercing acidity and sophisticated layers of flavor. We're not talking sugary Blue Nun type sweetness here, but something much more complex, sour sweet, difficult to pin down, tangy and mineral, offset by a honeyed richness.

The problem—the huge problem—is that Kabinett, Spätlese, Auslese, Beerenauslese and Trockenbeerenauslese are classifications awarded according to how sweet the fruit is when it's picked, and only that. They are NOT a sweetness indicator for the finished wine. Thus, although most Kabinetts are tangy and dry, and most Spätleses richer and fruitier (but still tangy and dry), some Kabinetts are richer and fruitier than some Spätleses which have been made in a dry style. So yes, the system is pretty useless as it stands—certainly in terms of consumer information, and most definitely in terms of choosing wines to go with foods. Unless you know your region and producer well, it's almost impossible to know which way a particular Kabinett or Spätlese is going to jump.

Efforts have already been made to try to clarify matters. Some modern wines are even labeled Dry, in English. Some wineries have taken their own steps by doing away with the old labeling, replacing it with a village name, or even a brand name and a varietal, in the New World style. Much more needs to be done. At the moment there is no real quality control or appellation system. This leads to immense confusion which doesn't do German wine's international standing any favors.

The unique character of German wine should be its strong selling point, but many German wineries are bowing to international pressures and producing drier and less distinctive stuff. The "Relaunch wines" which first came out in 1996 and are still being launched even now, and which are supposedly the beginning of a fresh new start for German wine, are meant to be drier, more balanced, more international, and more mass market in style. They stick at the $6–$8 price level, and come in French-shape bottles. Some are okay, but none are great. Few are even good.

Too many dull grape varieties have been planted in Germany, and the producers over-produce to a massive extent. When yields are too high, masses of dilute, inferior wine are the result. The dull workhorse white grape Müller-Thurgau was always the most common vine grown, but Riesling has now overtaken it in planted hectares, which has to be a good sign. Good Rieslings manage to pull off the hardest trick in the winemakers' book: however dry and tart they are, there's a richness of fruit underneath that's breathtaking. However rich and fruity they are, they contrive to be dry.

In general, don't bother with the reds. Unless you go to a specialist wine merchant, the German reds in most stores compare badly for quality and value with other countries of the world. Dornfelder, Spätburgunder (Pinot Noir) and Lemberger can be good from a top producer but quality examples are difficult to find. Stick with the Whites. If in doubt, stick with a Riesling Kabinett over $8. It's difficult to go wrong.

Cellaring: it's another slightly off-putting fact that lots of fine German wine needs a little bottle age. Lots of wine currently on sale is six or more years old—a fact that makes these bargain wines an even more extraordinary value. Some of these will need more bottle age. Riesling can age for 20, 30 years or more, at the highest level. Even some mid-priced wine needs 10–15 years. Yet at the other end of the scale a wine like Armand Riesling 1999 is drinking wonderfully well already, and most of the 1993 and 1994 wine currently on sale is in perfect drinking condition. Kabinetts are safest for fairly youthful tippling; Spätlese or Auslese is more likely to need bottle age. Even some wine of more modest origins, drinking well now, will age and improve in bottle. Rieslings have a wonderful ability to develop and flower into something new over time rather like fine Burgundy. The big difference is that there's very little good Burgundy available at $10 a bottle. In fact none.

Language of the Label: *Gutsabfüllung* or *Erzeuger-abfüllung* Estate bottled; *Rotwein* Red wine; *Weinbaugebiet* Wine region; *Weißherbst* Pink wine made from red grapes; *Eiswein* Made from grapes that have frozen solid. In making Eiswein, the water is separated out and the great concentration of the remaining fruit makes for intense, luscious wine. Sometimes the grapes are picked as late as January.

HANDY TIP: Wine labels featuring the word Bereich are usually to be avoided. It means "from the area of" the name that follows; thus Bereich Niersteiner trades on the Nierstein name and in so doing does it a grave disservice. Bereich wine is almost always bad news.

ANOTHER HANDY TIP: Because most German wines have ridiculously long and convoluted names almost impossible to remember when you actually get to the store, it's heartening to know that in Germany, it's the producers that are important. Producers are far more important than vintages: weather conditions are rarely ideal in the German climate so it's very much down to how estates manage the growing season (cold) and the harvest (wet and cold). Some good producers: Bürklin-Wolf, Deinhard, Dr. Loosen, Gunderloch, Kendermann, Von Bühl, Von Kesselstatt, Stüdert-Prüm, JJ Prum, Donnhof, Kunstler, Wittman and Müller-Catoir.

VINTAGES

Rain dashed hopes of 2000 being a good year, especially in the Mosel. There will be very little sweet wine and quantity is way down on 1999 everywhere. 1999 has proved to be an excellent Riesling year. 1998 was very good, 1997 warm and fleshy, '96 pretty good, as was '95. 1994 was ok, good for sweet wine, '93 good, '92 patchy, '91 small, and the '88/'89/'90 trio classic. 1984 was the last really atrocious year.

GRAPE VARIETIES
WHITES

Bacchus Usually dull, ripe, soft grape without much structure, but in the right hands nutty, savory, fresh and perfumy.

Gewürztraminer An Alsace speciality. Germany grows a little.

Grauburgunder *see* **Ruländer**

Huxelrebe On a good day this has many fine Riesling-like qualities, particularly in the Spätlese style. Wines are ripely green and fresh; Ausleses have added honeyed complexity.

Kerner One of the newer German grapes, bred by crossing Riesling with the native red Trollinger. Becoming popular in Rheinhessen particularly. Can seem obvious compared to Riesling but capable of producing fat, fresh, flavorsome wines.

Müller-Thurgau aka Rivaner Some of the top producers show what can be done with this otherwise dull, sweetish grapey grape, the bulk white staple of cheap bulk wine like Liebfraumilch. Germany's most grown grape until Riesling overtook it recently.

Pinot Gris *see* **Ruländer**

Riesling The star grape. Made well, has the complexity, fruit, acidity, and wonderful aromas that make a white wine truly memorable: perhaps with peach and green fruit, lemon and mineral character, with voluptuous ripeness and touches of steel. Riesling also makes stunningly good, complex dessert wines, with great richness, but undercut by refreshing acidity. New Wave examples like Ruppertsberg are clean, fruit-driven and off-dry, competent but not a little dull. Look out for Grans Fassian at your local wine shop.

🍷 Ruppertsberg Riesling
🍷🍷 Grans Fassian Riesling

Riesling Kabinett The Ockfener- (name of the village producing the wine) wine has amazing quality and quiet complexity for under $8. The Armand Riesling has layers of flavor and sophistication, a perfect summer white.

🍷 Ockfener Bockstein Riesling Kabinett, State Domaine Trier
🍷🍷 Armand Riesling Kabinett • Bernkasteler Badstube Riesling Kabinett • S A Prum Wehlener Sonnenuhr Riesling Kabinett • Forster Pechstein Riesling Kabinett, von Buhl
🍷🍷🍷 Scharzhofberger Kabinett, Egon Muller

Riesling Spatlese The Urziger wine is an extreme bargain at around $9, being medium sweet, but also serious and complex and totally delicious.

🍷🍷 Urziger Würzgarten Spätlese, Christoffel Berres •

Erdener Treppchen Riesling Spätlese • Johannisberger
Klaus Riesling Spätlese, Schloss Schonborn • Bernkasteler
Badstube Riesling Spätlese
🍷🍷🍷 Wehlener Sonnenuhr Riesling Spätlese

Riesling Auslese Ausleses vary, from the rich and pud-
dingy to the honeyed and yet fresh, with a background
piercing acidity. They all share a delicious fatness and
fullness of style, making them ideal aperitif and dessert
wines. Excellent with the cheeseboard.
🍷🍷 Mehringer Zellerberg Auslese • Waldracher Krone
Riesling Auslese, Peter Scherf
🍷🍷🍷 Wehlener Sonnenuhr Riesling Auslese

Rivaner *see* **Müller-Thurgau**

Ruländer aka Pinot Gris Called Ruländer when it's
dense and rich, perhaps slightly honeyed; called
Grauburgunder when made dry. The more international label Pinot Gris is now starting to appear on
export bottles. The Villa Wolf wine ($9) is both hon-
eyed and dry, herbal and rich.
🍷🍷 Villa Wolf Pinot Gris, Dr. Loosen, Pfalz

Scheurebe Green and harsh when unripe, but round,
ripely grapefruity, perhaps honeyed with firm, peppery
spice and orange fruit when properly ripened.

Silvaner Germany's third white grape after Riesling
and Müller-Thurgau. Can be good but it needs a top
producer. Shines in Franken; good from parts of

Rheinhessen and Baden. Otherwise, can lack flavor and acidity.

🍷🍷🍷 Silvaner Auslese Kronsberg ($18) half

Weissurgunder Can be creamy, nutty with peach and toffee. Little seen in the UK.

REDS

Dornfelder There are two styles: one fruity, jammy and light, the other barrel-aged, richer and intended for keeping. The good stuff has tremendous texture and style.

🍷🍷 Dornfelder Pfalz, Lergen Müller

Spätburgunder aka Pinot Noir Usually thin and unappetizing in the past, but good from top producers. Now Germany's third most grown grape variety, after Riesling and Müller-Thurgau.

🍷🍷 Spätburgunder Weinhaus Heger

WINE REGIONS

Ahr Tiny northerly region on a Rhein river tributary. Focusing on Pinot Noir (Spätburgunder), with mixed success.

Baden A narrow strip between the Rhine valley and the Black Forest. Despite being more southerly than other regions, wine-making is more scattered here, though vineyard acreage is rapidly increasing. Lots of red is made and some fine Ausleses, fermented dry for a rich but clean effect. Riesling Kabinetts and Spätleses are vigorous and winey. This is one of the warmer German regions, southerly in position and with its own relatively mild climate.

Franken Franconian wine comes in almost round, ancient-looking bottles. We don't see much of it abroad. If you should happen to stumble over some, go for the Silvaner. The season's too short to grow Riesling, and it's one of the few places that Silvaner really shines.

Mittelrhein Tourist area of hills and castles. Some good Riesling is produced despite this.

Mosel Saar Ruwer Mosel, like the Rhein valley, is a northerly region where grapes would struggle to ripen if it weren't for the steeply cut south-facing terraces designed to maximize the sunshine. The slate-rich soil is said to lend the characteristic mineral quality to their fine white wines.

"For many critics and drinkers alike, Mosel Riesling is the finest in the world."

For many critics and drinkers alike, Mosel Riesling is the finest in the world. Riesling thrives on these slate soils, producing young wines with green edges, a grapey aroma, and mouth-filling tart, sweet flavors. The best are intense, piquant, delicate wines, serious but also very enjoyable to drink. They might have sweet pea and hyacinth aromas, and more than a touch of mineral character. Mature Mosel is golden, honeyed, and often faintly gasoliney (sounds bad, tastes good). Some good dry Mosel is made but the best wines have a touch of delicate, fleeting sweetness to them. Two of the best Mosel villages, Piesport and Bernkastel are both also known for terrible sugary whites, Piesporter Micheslberg and Bereich Bernkasteler—avoid these. Look out for wines from top villages Erden, Wehlen and Urzig.

The Saar's cool climate is difficult for ripening grapes, but good years produce steely, dry crisp and mineral whites. A good Saar is a wonderful thing but they are difficult to find. Ruwer is a tiny region, making delicate wines in good years, mouthpuckeringly acidic ones in bad.

Riesling Kabinett Tangy green fruit, quiet background richness, but firmly drying. Intensity, concentration, zesty Granny Smith zing, a semi-spritzy texture and serious pithy dryness are common in the youthful wines. Wines open and soften with age, and acquire complex pungency. Often they have a slightly off-putting play-doh or warm plastic nose.

Riesling Spätlese Wines have more rich fruit body but retain that superbly crisp, quenching acidity. Scharzhofberger is a renowned estate and its Spätlese is a waxy, Cox and Granny Smith apple and apricot delight, with the signature whiff of the gasoline can at the close.

Riesling Auslese More juicy fruit, more sweetness, but still undercut by freshness, and finished by a perfumey kerosene dryness.

Nahe Nahe is an underrated region and its Rieslings can be good, perhaps with the clean grapey intensity of a Mosel, but with more mineral character. More citrus and steel is commonplace; others have a strawberry and lime fruit quality underpinning zingy acids, and a subtly spiced dryness. Some Nahe Rieslings can prove hit and miss in quality, though. Dönnhof is a reliably good estate if you can find it. As in the Mosel and Rhein, between which the Nahe is sandwiched, some good dry wine can be found but wines with a touch of sweetness are the real stars. Bargains are to be found here.

Pfalz Previously Rheinpfalz. Germany's big vineyard, 50 miles long, just to the north of Alsace. A sunny dry climate (along with Baden, Germany's warmest), protected by mountains, makes this an ideal venue for the German New Wave. An experimental attitude and bold new ventures with neglected varieties produce lots of good value wine. There's decent Scheurebe, good "Burgunders" and some pretty good red, much of it better than wine from the trendier Baden. Among the innovators and new arrivals there's a pocket of old-fashioned excellence: companies like von Bühl and Bürklin-Wolf are at the center of this Riesling-dominated region. These are succulent, voluptuous wines, solar-powered by fruit, and not the green, steely thrillers of the Mosel-Saar-Ruwer. But Pfalz is also home to considerable numbers of stinkers, many misguidedly conjured up for the sake of newness.

Grauburgunder A heavyweight Pinot Gris with a full, round, spiced-peaches character and vigorous acidity.

Kerner Pfalz Kerner makes some of the best summer whites around, if you can find wines with enough acid and dryness to balance the upfront fruit and cream.

Müller-Thurgau Müller-Thurgau is almost always a Liebfraumilchy letdown, but good modern ones (countable on one hand at present, admittedly) have good grapey flavors and a light touch that's very appealing. Look out for wines by Messmer.

Riesling New Wave dry Rieslings are still hit and miss, mostly miss, and their $6 price tag gives them away. The best have good fresh tangy flavors and an echo of Riesling complexity though most are simply clean, dry and smooth.

Riesling Kabinett Riesling Kabinetts from the Pfalz vary, some lean, grapefruity and tingly on the palate; others peachier and riper, though still fresh and spritzy. Often they combine limey sourness with cream and nut flavors and a fruit-skin dryness that's almost champagne-like.

Riesling Spätlese Pfalz Spätleses can be the most comforting, ripe and luscious of wines: rich, densely fruity, peppered by spice, warmed by tropical character, and cut through with lemon. Lively acids mean these wines can go on improving in bottle for 8–10 years.

New Wave Riesling The Pfalz is the HQ of the German New Wave. Wines have an international look, with French bottle shape and English labels. They have names like Devil's Rock and Fire Mountain. They come in two basic kinds: grapefruity, spritzy, a little on the crude side, or fuller-bodied, with lemon and tropical touches. Both sorts have the requisite dry finish the international style demands. Neither is really worth bothering with.

Scheurebe Good ones are deliciously round and ripe with orange notes amidst the rich grapeness and Cox apple crispness. There's often something Christmassy in there—a whiff of cloves amidst the satsuma aromas. Messmer is a good name.

Stickies The warm Pfalz can turn out good dessert wines. The best Beerenauslese wines are superb, both voluptuous and drying, seamlessly introducing fruits like kumquats, lemons and toffee into their clean, pleasantly alcoholic palate, and finishing with great tang, zing and style.

RHEINGAU

This wide fertile river valley is reasonably warm and dry, and 80% of the wine made here is Riesling. Some of the most famous estates in Germany are in this region, and Rheingau Rieslings are traditionally thought to be among the best in Germany. Despite this, or because of it, the region can seem complacent and over-priced. The Riesling style here is more robust and vigorous, contrasting with the delicate charm of Mosel. Traditionally this was an area for ripe, rich sweet wines but fashion has decreed that they be drier. Often they also have a background mineral salts note. Hochheim make a *halbtrocken* (off-dry) wine that manages to be complex, tantalizing and grassy with a delicious freshness ($9).

RHEINHESSEN

Janus-faced, this region. Most of its wine is bulk Müller-Thurgau and Silvaner for cheap export bottles, including millions of cases of Liebfraumilch. Nierstein has come to be associated with dreadful cheap bulk wine (Niersteiner Gutes Domtal) but in fact the Nierstein area produces some of the best fruit in Germany. Go for the expensive, single estate stuff, and not the Bereich Niersteiner though. Rheinhessen is also beginning to produce some good varietal wine. Only ten percent of the wine grown is Riesling.

Bacchus Look out for Wittmann's Bacchus, a zingy, savory hazelnut and elderflower cordial delight, sweet notes lingering at the back of the soft dry finish.

Huxelrebe Wittmann is also the acknowledged Huxelrebe specialist, managing to impart rich depths of Granny Smith fruit into his tastebud-rousing, superzingy Huxelrebe Spätlese. The Huxelrebe Auslese maintains its grapefruit zing but overlays it with honeyed richness.

Kerner Good Kerner exhibits the true individuality of the grape, with its creamy but sharp, almost goats cheesy flavors, and subtle, smoky dried-apricot fruit.

Riesling It's possible to find mature Riesling at low prices, with softly, sweetly gasoline-tinged greengage fruit, preserved-lemon flavors, fresh acids and a spicy ginger finish. Some Riesling manages to be both rich but also as drying as grapefruit pith, with gooseberry, green apple and sour kiwi fruit.

Stickies Rheinhessen dessert wines can compete with the best in Germany at bargain prices.

WÜRTTEMBERG

Usually lumped with Baden. Some good reds (Lemberger particularly), and lots of more ordinary wine are made here, but few (if any) make it abroad. The locals love their thin red Trollinger reds; outsiders fail to see their charm. A little decent Riesling is also made.

ITALY

Look at Italy on the map, and it's a great long sinuous mass of hill-slopes, with a huge variety of microclimates suiting different grape varieties—mountainous with Alpine influences in the north, extremely hot in the Mediterranean south and on the islands. Given the patchwork of soils and slopes, geology and sunny climate, this is a country made for wine-growing. It's still the number one country for volume. It's also extremely traditional in approach, or rather was until recently. Italy is on the up, on a roll, and getting seriously into technology.

Italy has always made plenty of good quality wine, but the names we know best are the bulk export wines: Lambrusco, Soave, Orvieto and Frascati. On the Red side, perhaps Valpolicella, or Chianti. All wines we've known and had a love-hate relationship with for 30 years at least, and still stuck in a 1970s timewarp, many of them. Lambrusco is Italy's Liebfraumilch, and does a similar disservice to its reputation abroad. With one proviso. Real Lambrusco, the sort drunk on holiday in a heat-baked square, is a delicious wine. It's just the stuff made in bulk and shipped out to gullible Americans that's so dreadful.

The last edition of the *Wine Guide* was quite categorical. "To find wine with character and flavor, DON'T BUY anything labeled Lambrusco, Orvieto or Frascati, and only buy Soave and Valpolicella from a good producer." None of these, it was written, do justice to an amazingly diverse wine nation. This is still true, on the whole, but . . . Things are changing. The occasional real Lambrusco (it's expensive) is popping up in the better wine shops. One or two surprising, New Wave Soaves and Orvietos have reached American shores. There's more and more decent Valpolicella about. Even a drinkable Frascati or two. Though it has to be said that most of the good cheap Italian wine doesn't come from any of these appellations, but from more obscure corners of the country, and overwhelmingly, from the south and Sicily.

Until recently, Italy has been easy to write off as a white wine producer. Italy's most planted white grape, Trebbiano, is also Italy's dullest, being over-cropped, bland and barely worth the bother of opening the bottle. Pinot Grigio is usually equally dull, but there are signs of dramatic improvement here. Italian producers are putting more effort into smartening up their traditional varieties and finding, as many other winemakers have the world over, that a New World makeover of an old winery can make a phenomenal difference. Even a not-very-radical New Wave tweak of how things are done can make a huge impact on the quality and flavor of wines. Previously rather dull appellations like Verdicchio dei Castelli di Jesi are now turning out masses of delicious, newly focused white.

The Italian preference is still for whites so bland as to be barely there; subtle, fresh, mineral-watery wine with pared-back fruit. But partly because of the demands of export markets, there are now increasing numbers of fuller-bodied, richer-flavored whites. Sometimes this is down to blending their own grapes with new arrivals like Chardonnay and Sauvignon (or making straight French varietals), sometimes it's down to changing the way they grow and make their traditional whites, with lower yields, use of stainless steel and new French or American oak. As far as reds go, many still fall into an Italian groove, with soft cherry fruit and a bitter dry twist. The bigger reds often show more of the same, in greater concentration—richer cherry fruit, more bitter almond, along with hefty oak and alcohol. Remember that Italians expect to eat with wine, and many wines are made accordingly, to cope with Italian food. But there are changes afoot here too. New wave methods are bringing more fruit and freshness. Foreign grape varieties, particularly Cabernet Sauvignon, are making a huge impact, particularly in blending.

> "The Italian preference is still for whites so bland as to be barely there ..."

It can be tricky finding your way around. If in doubt,
stick with wines from the south (Puglia, Sicily) where
the New Wave is most active, making good robust characterful reds and, despite the heat, some delicious
whites too, including masses of good Chardonnay and
Chardonnay-native blends. But even in the marketing-
savvy south, what's especially cheering about Italian
wine culture is that despite the lure of Chardonnay,
Cabernet and friends, this is still very much a traditional wine country, which loves its many quirky native
grapes and is concentrating most of its effort on
improving what's Italian, rather than ripping it all out
and planting with international grape varieties.

Italian wine labels can be a nightmare. Names are
confusing and can appear arbitrary. It's often difficult
to find a recognizable region or any point of familiarity at all. The DOC system both helps and hinders.
DOC (appellation contrôlée, in effect) and DOCG
(theoretically a step up) can point the way to good
stuff, but not always. DOC was so restricting until its
recent overhaul that many of the best producers had
no choice but to label their wines *Vino da Tavola* (table
wine). They were good wines, but made outside the
regulations. This led to the phenomenon of the Super
Tuscans: vino da tavola of DOCG standard, at high
prices. Despite the overhaul of the system in 1992,
which should have sorted out the classification fiasco
(good Italian word that) but didn't really, some high
class Vino da Tavola is still made—though most is
basic, rustic and inferior. Opting to be of Vino da
Tavola status is a radical decision that only those confi-

dent of their fan-club could contemplate. Vino da
Tavola regulations don't permit the mention of region,
variety or vintage on the label.

In addition to DOC and DOCG, there is now IGT,
or Indicazione Geografica Tipica, in effect a Vin de
Pays system. Some DOC producers have opted for IGT
status as a matter of choice and as a form of protest,
objecting to the low standards or wrong-headed rules
of their official DOC. Or, like the Super-Tuscans, they
want to do something new which DOC regulations
won't permit. But none of this is really relevant. Forget
DOC, DOCG and IGT and look instead to the producer or vineyard name.

Language of the Label: *Bianco* white; *Rosso* red; *Nero*
dark red; *Chiaretto* light red; *Rosaro* pink; *Secco* dry;
Amaro very dry/bitter; *Dolce* sweet; *Spumante* fizzy;
Frizzante spritzy; *Passito* from dried, concentrated
fruit; *Recioto* half-dried out, concentrated and sweet;
Tenuta estate/property; *Vendemmia* vintage; *Riserva*
oak-aged, usually 3 years minimum; *Classico* from the
best area (supposedly).

VINTAGES

The 2000 harvest brought extreme weather conditions; intense heat meant an exceptional year for
reds. It was a good year for the south in general,
and for Piedmont. 1999 was an excellent year, '98
patchy, '97 fleshy and mixed, and '96 good for
whites and for Piedmont. 1995 and '90 were also
excellent years. 1992, '93 and '94 were patchy.

GRAPE VARIETIES
WHITES

Arneis Old, quirky white variety. Apples, pears and spice.

Chardonnay Traditionally, lean, fresh and unoaked, though creamier, yeastier Barrique (barrel-made) wines are becoming more popular.

Cortese White grape of Piedmont. Dry, citric, can be good.

Falanghina Apparently the favorite white of Ancient Rome. Can be rich, well-textured, cakey, almost Sémillon-like. Has great potential.

Garganega The Soave grape. Generally bland, soft and appley, but a revelation in the right hands.

Gewürztraminer Most is actually Traminer, a lesser variety. True Gewürztraminer is good in the far north.

Grechetto Plump, spicy, hazel-nutty white, helps add character to Trebbiano-based blends.

Greco Crisp, minerally, can be bland.

Malvasia Nutty and creamy white, good in blends.

Moscato Germanic Moscato varietals can be deliciously musky and fragrant in the far north. Terrific in Asti, where it makes deliciously sherbety, grapey fizz.

Müller-Thurgau, Rheinriesling, Sylvaner German varietals are grown up in the Alpine foothills of the Alto Adige, but are rarely very interesting.

Pinot Bianco Okay in the Alto Adige and Friuli, where it's mild, but plump and softly honeyed.

Pinot Grigio aka Pinot Gris Subtle, crisp whites. Too subtle usually but New Wave producers are turning the grape's poor reputation around.

Sauvignon Blanc Subtle, green, crisp whites from the north and northeast, but also grown further south. Generally dull.

Tocai Northeastern white grape. Can be good; dry, nutty and waxy.

Trebbiano Usually bad news: a bland but prolific white grape responsible for lots of very dull bland wine. In France Trebbiano is called Ugni Blanc and is largely confined to Armagnac production and to Gascon country whites.

Verdicchio Crisp, lemony, nutty fish whites from the Adriatic coast.

REDS

Barbera Red staple of Piedmont and the northwest. Can be dark, drying, plummy and redcurrant-tart, and is often best made very simply. Sour sweetness and raisin flavors are common.

Bonarda Plump, plummy, can have cocoa and prune flavors.

Cabernet Franc Now common in the northeast. Juicy, sappy reds.

Cabernet Sauvignon Used in the northeast and Tuscany, often for blending. Now being grown as a single varietal and for blends in the New Wave Italian south, with increasing conviction and success.

Cannonau Red Sardinian relative of Grenache.

Dolcetto Soft, easy, fleshy, cherryish, but also dry, perhaps bitter.

Malvasia Nera Dark fruity variety much used in the south.

Merlot Found in Tuscany and central Italy, mostly in red blends, but can be good as a varietal in the northeast.

Montepulciano Fruity, herby, drying red, still under-appreciated.

Nebbiolo Italy's big red grape. Wines are usually tannic, and need bottle age. Smoky and sweet, fruity and leathery, earthy and rich.

Negroamoro and Nero d'Avola Southern reds of rich fruit, herb-edged and characterful in the right hands. Often used in blending. Negroamoro (Puglia) is often raisin-edged and can be port-like in its rich alcoholic sweetness. Nero d'Avola (Sicily) is damson-fruited and gently savory.

Primitivo Rich and spicy fruity reds in the south. The grape elsewhere known as Zinfandel.

Sangiovese Italy's most planted red grape. Important in Tuscany, where it's the main Chianti grape. A chameleon, rich and herby, or soft and tart. Easily identified by its herbal edge, with notes of orange zest and tea.

REGIONS

THE NORTHWEST

Piemonte (Piedmont) Famous for its clean white Spumantes (Asti, Moscato d'Asti). Barolo and Barberesco are its two prime reds, both made from Nebbiolo. They are the only two known by their village name; otherwise it's varietals like Barbera and Dolcetto. Wines can add a village name if they are from a specific area, like Barbera d'Asti. Local white grape variety Arneis is now being produced as a single varietal. Gavi Cortese is a popular white in Italy, fêted as a sort of local Chablis.

Lombardy Barbera dominates the Oltrepò DOC reds, usually with Bonarda to make up the volume. Oltrepò whites are often from the Pinot family. Moscato is also made.

THE NORTHEAST

The heartland of the northern New Wave, and home to some more established household names, like Soave and Valpolicella (in **Veneto**). Bardolino reds are light and on a better day also juicy. Bianco di Custoza whites also come from Veneto. **Trentino/Aldo Adige** cosies up to the Alps and is otherwise known as Sud Tirol; **Friuli Venezie Giulia** snuggles up to the coast. Lots of crisp white varietals are being made in the cool mountain foothills, and some light reds. Cabernet Franc is proving successful. Vineyards in Alto Adige, Italy's most northerly, produce good German varieties like Gewürztraminer and Silvaner.

The large region of **Emilia Romagna** straddles the country between the northeast corner and Tuscany. This is the home of dull (in some cases dreadful) export wines like Lambrusco. Lambrusco can be a drinkable wine—if you drink it in Italy, where it's

likely to be youthful, very fresh and slightly tart. Lambrusco made for the export market is merely sweet and
pappy.

CENTRAL ITALY

Tuscany Home of Chianti. The famous Brunello, in
the southern belt, is very late picked from old vines
with low yields. It's slow-fermented and then barrel-
aged for a minimum of four years. Vino Nobile di
Montepulciano is made from Chianti ingredients, but
spends a minimum of two years in barrel. The idea is
that it's a more serious, sophisticated red. Often,
though, it's just a hard, closed-up, over-oaked one.

Umbria is the home of Orvieto, a wine that, like Lambrusco, is a lot more interesting when you drink it on
its home turf. Traditionally it was a sweet wine, but in
its modern guise is barely there at all, other than having a buttery, nutty twist to its limpid lemon fruit (if
you're lucky). Montefalco reds can be very fine.

Marches on the east coast produces the increasingly
good white Verdicchio dei Castelli di Jesi, and Rosso
Conero reds. Lots of budget bulk wine is also turned
out, some of it surprisingly quaffable.

Abruzzi has an undervalued but often good red in its
Montepulciano d'Abruzzo; **Latium** makes the generally bland and spritzy Frascati.

THE SOUTH

Like other southern zones in Europe, most notably the south of France, the Italian south was previously thought to be suitable only for low-grade bulk wine, but is now waking up to its potential.

Puglia (Apulia) Traditionally, a bulk wine area mostly for domestic consumption, but Puglian DOCs are multiplying fast. Primitivo (Zinfandel) is at the heart of the Puglian red revival. Negroamoro makes roasted, slightly port-like reds. Salice Salentino, Copertino and Squinzano can be excellent.

Campania Some serious reds among the rustic stuff. Taurasi is good.

Sicily Recently the island vineyards have been outdoing Puglia for rich, easy, value reds. Own brand Sicilian Rosso can be a good cheap buy.

PICK OF APPELLATIONS, REGIONS, VARIETALS

Barberesco Fashionable, expensive, Nebbiolo reds. Big and complex, but also softly fruity and herby.

Barbera d'Asti In Piedmont. Barbera is the grape, Asti the place. Populist versions have lively, cherry, strawberry and plum fruit, and a drying finish with a little almond flavor. Wines can be resiny or have very dry chocolate raisin character.

🍷 Barbera Piemonte, Girelli • Albera Barbera d'Asti Superiore, Piemonte
🍷🍷 Barbera d'Asti Tabarin, Icardi

Bardolino Usually light, paleish chiaretto reds.

Barolo From Piedmont. Like Barberesco, Barolo is made from Nebbiolo, but wines tend to be beefier and chunky. Good ones are deeply, richly fruity (plums, cherries) with tobacco, chocolate and prune in support. They're much readier to drink young than they used to be. These are highly sought after snob wines and are priced accordingly. $20 is cheap.

🍷🍷🍷 Barolo La Mara • Barolo Costa di Bussia

Bianco di Custoza From Veneto. Zingy, often with more zing than flavor, maybe with a bitter apple-skins dryness on the finish. New Wave wines have richer flavor and texture, a subtle sherbet spritz and a nutty, lemony character, perhaps with lime and green olive. The single varietal Garganega is unusual but shows what a good, boldly fruity, hazelnut-finished wine this can be.

🍷 Bianco di Custoza, Gorgo • Terre in Fiore Garganega, Cantina di Custoza

Chianti Tuscan Sangiovese blends (though 100% Sangiovese wines exist) can be bitter and hard, with too-sour fruit. Classico wines aren't always the best. Good ones are generous, warm, with raspberry and cherry fruit, orange and savory notes, and more than a hint of strong tea, before closing with a firm nip of bitterness and spice. Some are too dry, leafy and muscular to drink without food. Chianti can seem a wretched appellation at times, trading more on its fame than for its quality.

 Melini Chianti

 Chianti Classico Teuzzo, Cecchi • Chianti Classico, Bianfi • Chianti Classico, La Torraccia di Presura • Chianti Classico, Castello La Lecchia

 Chianti Classico Riserva Rocca Guicciadia, Ricasoli

Dolcetto Huge improvements are being made with the modest Dolcetto grape. The Dogliani wine has rich fruit, plummy dry and elegant.

 Dolcetto d'Alba de Forville • Dolcetto di Dogliani, San Fereolo

Falanghina This southern grape variety smells of dried apricots and brown sugar. Flavors are more cakey (Danish pastry), but with rousing acidity and floral notes.

 Taburno Falanghina • Falanghina, Feudi di San Gregorio

Frascati The Latium region is little known but its bland spritzy wine Frascati was hugely popular 30 years ago. The occasional wine has flavor as well as bubbles, like this $6 bottle.

🍷 Frascati Superiore Tenuta delle Marmorelle

Friuli Light but juicy, tasty reds from the cool northeast corner. Friuli Grave is the biggest of the six areas. Decent quaffable varietal whites are also made.

Gavi There's lots going on in Piedmont and the whites especially can be cheeringly quirky, using the local Cortese grape variety. Gavi Cantine Gemma is lime-fruited, drying and floral in the mouth. La Chiara is more full-bodied, with great texture. Castello di Tassarolo is fresh, with creamy rice pudding aromas and an elegant, melon-tinged fruit. Wines are $9–$15. The Raccolto Tardivo wine is a late harvest sweetie.

🍷🍷 Gavi Cantine Gemma • Gavi, La Chiara • Gavi Castello di Tassarolo • Villa Lanata Gavi Raccolto Tardivo

Lugana One of the better Trebbiano DOCs. Zenato is the name to look out for. Villa Flora is a subtle but appealingly crisp and faintly melony refreshing summer white, good with salad.

🍷🍷 Lugana Villa Flora, Zenato

Montalcino Famous for its Brunello. Hefty oak aging can kill off the fruit in these big serious Sangioveses, but the survivors can seriously impress, with their sweet dense ripe fruit, and faintly brie-cheesey, savory, almond dryness. The effect can be that of a splendid edifice rather than something you'd actually want to drink. Rosso di Montalcino is the DOC for regular reds.

Montepulciano d'Abruzzo Good Montepulciano d'Abruzzo can mean good juicy, peppery food reds at a low price, though "designer" wines are also made. The pricier ones tend to be densely fruited, chocolatey, with herby dryness, and perhaps some pretty hefty tobacco-edged tannins. Look out for Barone Cornacchia wines, one of the New Wave of smaller producers from the northwest of the region.

🍷 Montepulciano d'Abruzzo Umani Ronchi • Barone Cornacchia Montepulciano d'Abruzzo

🍷🍷 Montepulciano d'Abruzzo, Vigna le Coste, Barone Cornacchia

🍷🍷🍷 Vino Nobile di Montepulciano, Avignonesi

Montepulciano—White High class Trebbiano does exist. This brand is a true New Wave wine, showing the potential of both region and varietal.

🍷🍷 Trebbiano d'Abruzzo Altare, Marramiero

Montepulciano—Vino Nobile Not from Abruzzi, but from Tuscany. Bigger, more serious (more expensive), or just a whole lot drier and harder to love, but otherwise not unlike its sibling Chianti.

Orvieto Umbria's best known white is almost always a neutral dry wine. Just occasionally, a good one turns up, with more fruit and texture. Often they have a drying finish and a touch of spritz.

🍷 Orvieto Tenuta Le Velette, Classico

Pinot Grigio Italian Pinot Gris is usually a bland, identical white, but it can shine up in the north, and is being turned out in volume in Trentino. Good ones are lemony and crisp, with zing and zest, a characteristic edge of peppery, herbal spice, gently savory like white peaches, and sometimes a fuller, fatter apricot note. Having said all that, most are pretty thin and subtle, but they make good summer refreshers.

🍷 La Via Pinot Grigio
🍷🍷 Trentino Pinot Grigio, Terraze della Luna

Puglia—Reds Puglian reds are the best cheap reds in Italy. (And cheap they are, too—the first wine listed below is just $4.50 a bottle.) Deeply berryish and ripe,

they often have a concentration of fruit and structure that belies their low cost. The best are from the hot peninsula of Salento. Wines can appear harsh and acidic at first; if so, pour and leave them (or do what the locals do and decant into a jug for table use). Wines bedevilled by bitter cherry, almond paste and alcohol are thus transformed into rich and ripe, plum and blackcurrant-fruited wines, with a drying finish. Others are more tomatoey, savory, slightly medicinal, great with garlicky food. Many Puglians are made from the juicy, spicy Primitivo (Zinfandel); Negroamoro and Malvasia Nera also make for substantial reds here. Sangiovese and Cabernet Sauvignon are becoming more popular. Low rainfall and intense heat in summer 2000 means the latest Puglian reds are better than ever, with intense berry flavors.

🍷 M&S Rosso di Puglia • Mezzomondo Rosso Salento Negroamaro • Puglia Primitivo Sangiovese • Bright Bros. Negroamaro Cabernet Sauvignon • Fantini Sangiovese • Primitivo del Salento, Antonini • Primitivo del Salento, San Crispino • Primitivo del Salento, Sigillo Primo • Promessa Rosso Salento

🍷🍷 Amativo Negroamaro Primitivo • Felline Albarello, Rosso del Salento

Puglia—Whites This hot region can overcompensate for its past tendency to produce big flabby monsters. Some of its lean and clean cold-fermented whites are effectively stripped of flavor: lemony, light, dry, mineral watery, with a capsicum bite, remarkably like a northern wine, in short.

🍷 Salice Salentino Bianco • Trulli Chardonnay, Salento

Sardinia Sardinia's hot sunshine can produce reds of

great intensity, though some are over-baked tasting. The glorious Carignano del Sulcis is drying and figgy but also generously fruity, with cocoa and spice, and that characteristically Italian marzipan and alcohol framework. The Costera Grenache (Cannonau) is rich and raisiny with a chocolate coating to its dark autumn fruits.

🍷🍷 Carignano del Sulcis • Costera, Cannonau di Sardegna Argiolas

Sicily—Reds A satisfying balance of rich, warming fruit, firm food-friendly tannins and a sweetish ripe note is the classic Sicilian recipe. Many have a dry savory-raisin edge, others are over-ripe and soupy. New World methods are producing more fresh, juicy reds at low prices, many of them macerated in stainless steel for more skin color and flavor. Some of these have hefty alcohol levels. Private brand Sicilian red can be a good budget buy. Brian Fletcher, the Australian behind the new Accademia del Sole range from Familia Sacco, has produced an exceptional wine here for just $8, rich, layered and sweetly fruited.

🍷 Il Padrino Rosso Sicilia • Il Padrino Sangiovese • Inycon Cabernet Sauvignon • Inycon Merlot • Accademia del Sole Calatrasi, Sangiovese Syrah

Sicily—Whites Despite the heat, the tradition here is for lean crisp whites, using native varietals like Grecanico and Catarratta, which brings a fleshier, peachy note. Kym Milne's Zagarra Catarratta Chardonnay blend has good weight and balance, lemons and herbs.

Chardonnay is now taking off in a big way in Sicily, encouraged by the Super-Sicilian, Planeta Chardonnay ($20 in the last edition, $27 in this), which has an international following. Barrel fermentation is the key—the newcomer Inycon Chardonnay is made in a big tropical style, buttery and alcoholic with melon and banana flavors.

🍷 Zagara Catarratta Chardonnay • Bright Bros. Sicilian Barrel Fermented Chardonnay • Inycon Chardonnay

🍷🍷🍷 Planeta Chardonnay

Soave New Wave examples like that from Coffele ($9.75) have radical richness of flavor and texture, but most Soave is still dreadfully bland. The Zenato wine has more flavor than the common herd, with baked apple fruit and crisp tanginess. Recioto (sweet) wines are also made.

🍷 Soave Classico Zenato

🍷🍷 Soave Classico Superiore, Coffele • Soave Classico, Pieropan

Trentino Trentino Chardonnays are usually green, crisp, mildly fruity, decidedly tangy. Like many Trentino wines they can also be dilute-tasting, thanks to too high yields. Some decent light and juicy red is also made.

Tuscany—Reds At its best, the Sangiovese is plummy, but perhaps plum-skin dry, fleshy with chocolate edges, juicy and lovable. Wines can be chunky, with slightly dusty, earthy fruit. The so-called Super-Tuscans

are frequently Cabernet Sauvignons. Prices can be distressingly high.

🍷 Col di Sasso, Banfi

🍷🍷 Centine Sant'Antimo Toscanna, Banfi • Rosso Toscano, Cantine Bonacchi • Dogajolo Carpineto Toscana

Tuscany—Whites Cecchi is a reliable name to go for. Tuscan whites can be surprisingly creamy, even at the budget end. There are lots of accomplished, very smart whites on offer too: Le Grance, a white Super-Tuscan, is a deliciously sophisticated blend of Chardonnay Sauvignon and Traminer.

🍷🍷🍷 Le Grance Vino Bianco Toscana da Tavola, Tenuta Caparzo

Valpolicella Has suffered a decline in status, but these soft, easy reds can be surprisingly good. Basic models have light cherry fruit and a softly bitter, cherry-stone dryness. Others have rich sweet fruit, a touch of almond/marzipan and bags of charm.

🍷 Valpolicella Classico Zenato

Valpolicella Amarone These rich wines made from half-dried-out grapes can be stunningly good. They are big and dry but also rich with fruit. Recioto wines are sweet.

♟♟♟ Amarone delle Valpolicella Classico Rocca Sueva • Amarone delle Valpolicella Tedeschi • Amarone delle Vapolicella Zenato

Valpolicella Ripasso In the Ripasso method the young wine is passed over the Recioto Amarone lees and skins for extra body and oomph. The results are delicious.

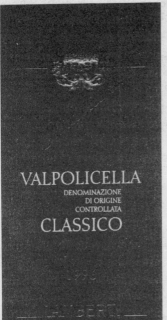

♟♟ Valpolicella Ripasso La Caseta de Ettore Righetti, Classico

Valpolicella Rosata Pink wines are also made in Valpolicella. The Arcadia wine is made in a modern fruit-driven style, fresh, crisp and drying on the finish.

♟ Arcadia Rosata, Veronese

Veneto Forward-looking region with New Wave influences, though red cheapies can follow the traditional cherries-and-almonds model. This is

VALPOLICELLA
DENOMINAZIONE
DI ORIGINE
CONTROLLATA
CLASSICO

also the home of one of the world's great stickies, in
Maculan Torcolato.

Verdicchio dei Castelli di Jesi Traditionally lean and
subtle fish whites, but New Wave Verdicchio has a
richer flavor and texture, typically with a spicy buttery
character (barrel fermentation is taking off here). The
Villa Bianchi wine is one such. Others are more subtle,
with a clean fresh spritzy character. Excellent seafood
and all-purpose summer whites at bargain prices.

🍷 Verdicchio dei Castelli di Jesi, Collelungo • Verdicchio dei
Castelli di Jesi, Coste del Molino • Verdicchio dei Castelli di
Jesi, Moncaro • Verdicchio dei Castelli di Jesi, Villa Bianchi

NEW ZEALAND

New Zealand says its big story is the vast improvement in its reds, and that it is diversifying its whites, away from Sauvignon and Chardonnay. To the hapless wine-buyer, it seems that the big story is really the continuing rise in prices, especially for reds, and that despite proclamations of love for Riesling, Pinot Gris and other less obvious white varietals, Sauvignon Blanc and Chardonnay still outnumber other whites by ten to one at least.

But to give New Zealand some credit, it is certainly true that like Australia, the country is getting more interested in growing wine, rather than just making it. Vineyard acreage has doubled in the last ten years. Like Australia, producers here are now very interested in producing wines with class. Huge winery giant Montana still rules the New Zealand scene, and makes excellent wine of all kinds and colors, but there are also lots of dedicated little producers striving for individuality. Like Montana, they are improving vineyard sites, looking to diversify with lots of experimental planting, and are mad for technology—all designed to extract as much fruit, color and flavor out of their wines as possible in a fairly challenging climate.

New Zealand isn't a hot country, but even in the cooler districts, a long, long growing season means the fruit ripens slowly and flavors intensify. Vines grow very happily in its big stony valleys. Good soil, good climate, good winemakers . . . sounds like a paradise for wine. There's only one serious fly in the ointment: the weather. The last ten years has been bedevilled by disastrously cold wet summers. The upshot has been wine shortages, price rises, (1999 and 2000 were good years, but prices are still rising) and a spate of rough, under-ripened reds. This means that vintages are more important in New Zealand than in any other New World country. It's the New World zone that most approximates to Europe in its vintage dependency, especially for red wine.

As far as red wine trends are concerned, more Pinot Noir and Merlot has been planted. They are cooling off on Cabernet Sauvignon a bit (difficult to ripen), and using it more in blends to compensate for its problems. Malbec is the coming thing. Hawkes Bay is still the red area to watch; despite weather problems, wines are improving fast here, as a result of better vineyard management. But it all comes at increasing cost. Prices are getting silly for New Zealand reds. They must, like California, have a dedicated following, convinced the quality and individuality of these wines is such that price hikes can be tolerated. On a good day it's easy to see this—especially for Pinot Noir, which costs a fortune anywhere if it comes close to Burgundy quality. Mostly, though, New Zealand reds just seem overpriced. It's now commonplace to spend $13 on a fairly ordinary New Zealand red. Why bother, when the world is awash with good ripe wine at much lower prices?

White wine is still the main point of New Zealand, which made its name with its extraordinary, gooseberryish Sauvignon Blanc—it's difficult to overstate the impact those ripe grassy pea-pod and asparagus wines made when they burst onto the scene 20 years ago. It seemed like they had reinvented the Sauvignon grape. World demand went whoosh and the Loire fell over in a dead faint. In the last five years Chardonnay has become more important. But New Zealand now declares itself bored with both these whites. The home market appears to be turning to wines with sweetness and spice. Riesling is now the most fashionable white, and Pinot Gris is rising fast. Masses of misconceived Müller-Thurgau is being grubbed up (early advisors, as in English vineyards, said this was the German grape to plant—it's vigorous and hardy—but they forgot to add that it doesn't taste of anything).

VINTAGES
2000 was an excellent year, particularly for Sauvignon and Riesling, though quantity was lower than hoped for. Reds were patchier—cellar those Pinot Noirs. 1998 and '99 were better for Reds; '98 in particular was too warm for really good white,

and was a superb red year. 1997 was down in
quantity but Marlborough whites were very fine.
1996 was pretty good for whites and for Hawkes
Bay reds. 1995 was generally poor, the last of a trio
of poor years, especially difficult for reds.

REGIONS

AUCKLAND

The original center of the New Zealand wine business,
on the North Island, further north than Gisborne and
Hawkes Bay. It's common to make wine with imported
fruit from other areas. The Auckland appellation also
includes a host of sub-regions, like Waiheke Island,
thought by many to be perfect NZ "claret" vineyards.

GISBORNE

Covers the whole area around Poverty Bay, which is
north of Hawkes Bay on the east coast of the North
Island. Gisborne is the home of excellent Chardonnay,
and other white varietals—even Gewürztraminer,
though this is a comparatively warm area. In general
stick to the Chardonnay. It's too warm here for much
good Sauvignon; wines can taste over-ripe and blowsy,
lacking in Sauvignon freshness, though blends can be
good. Some decent Chardonnay Semillon blends are
produced, though cheap over-cropped ones risk tasting merely tropical and dull. Good single varietal
Chenin Blanc is made if you can find it. This can also

risk being fat and tropical, appley and dull (like lots of South African wine) though the high class ones have a dry sour yeasty quality that makes them age well. Reds are also made.

HAWKES BAY

Hawkes Bay, on the eastern coast of the North Island is New Zealand's next big thing. Not that it's a new region—wine has been grown and made here for over 100 years. Many established producers are buying a slice; lots of fruit is carted off elsewhere to distant wineries. This is a warm region, and has become the focus for the production of good quality reds, particularly Cabernet Sauvignon and Merlot. Good quality whites are also emerging. This is now a hugely popular Chardonnay zone, New Zealand's trendiest. Chardonnays are richer and riper than the Marlborough model, but retain a crisp balancing acidity. Some Sauvignon Blanc is also made, lusher, green-beany, yeastier than the Marlborough classic: most tastes over-ripe, lacking in good varietal character. Hawkes Bay would be the hippest region in NZ if it weren't for the Pinot Noir gold-rush going on in Marlborough, and the current fashion for Riesling.

"Hawkes Bay . . . is New Zealand's next big thing."

MARLBOROUGH

Traditionally wine was grown and made around Auckland. In just 20 years Marlborough, at the cool, windy, northern tip of the South Island, has become New Zealand's biggest wine-growing area, famous for its world-beating gooseberry, asparagus, grass Sauvignon Blanc-style. Other regions make Sauvignon, but none comes close. Chardonnay can be good, though it tends to be on the lean and tangy side; first Gisborne, and now Hawkes Bay have stolen the thunder with their own richer, riper, creamier Chardonnay styles. But Rieslings are now hugely fashionable and Marlborough is the place for them. Pinot Gris is being planted here too. But the big Marlborough story is the red story. Though Marlborough has trouble ripening Cabernet Sauvignon and Merlot, which have become Hawkes Bay varieties, Pinot Noir has proved to be another Marlborough specialty. Awatere Valley, to the south of Marlborough, is an impressive new sub-region.

"Marlborough ... is famous for its world-beating gooseberry, asparagus, grass Sauvignon Blanc-style."

MARTINBOROUGH

Part of the Wairarapa region on the North Island, a cool district now famous for its smash hit red. Martinborough also produces white varietals like Sauvignon, which tend to have more ripe fruit and tropical notes than the classic Marlborough wine. This is a boutique vineyard area with high priced, low-yield, much-sought-after wines, none more highly thought of than its Pinot Noir, which has started a New Zealand "red burgundy" gold-rush thanks to its international reputation. Good, if expensive, Chardonnays are also made.

OTHER REGIONS

Nelson, just west of Marlborough on the South Island, has enormous potential as a cool climate zone. Canterbury, further south, is up and coming, as is its Waipara sub-region. Central Otago, a cold region down in the depths of the South Island at the very southern tip of the wine-growing belt, is planting lots of Pinot Noir.

GRAPE VARIETIES

WHITES

Chardonnay Gisborne wines were the thing five years ago. Now it's Hawkes Bay. Prices are going up and it's difficult to find good wine on a budget; Sanctuary and In the Black are the only two sub-$10.50 bottles here.

¶¶ The Sanctuary Chardonnay • In the Black Chardonnay • Oyster Bay Chardonnay • Villa Maria Chardonnay • Montana Gisborne Barrel-Fermented Chardonnay • Villa Maria Cellar Selection Chardonnay • Delegat's Reserve Chardonnay, Hawkes Bay • Montana McDonald Church

Road Chardonnay, Hawkes Bay • Te Mata Chardonnay
🍷🍷🍷 Craggy Range Chardonnay, Hawkes Bay • Church
Road Reserve Chardonnay • Elston Chardonnay, Te Mata,
Hawkes Bay

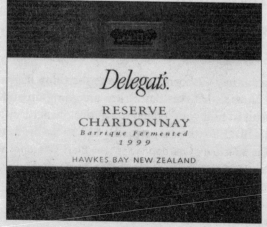

Chenin Blanc Is NZ's flirtation with Chenin Blanc over? The few that make it abroad are generally grassy, lanolin-edged and hard, in need of bottle age. But better that than the vacuous apple fruit of warm climate Chenin.

Gewurztraminer Gaining ground as the fashion for spicy, sweeter wines takes hold. Wines currently cost $12 and over.

🍷🍷 Montana Reserve Gewurztraminer

Pinot Gris Can make good, plump wines with a hint of white peach flavor and pepper. New Zealand wines tend to be riper and fleshier than is common in the spicier European model.

🍷🍷 Shingle Peak Pinot Gris, Marlborough

Riesling The grape of the year. Masses of new vineyards are coming on line. Wines are getting more sophisticated and can age well, though cheap ones are still fairly simple, fruity and tangy. Buy up those year 2000 wines, they are very impressive. The Villa Maria wine, at just $9, has lemon and lime acidity, structure, freshness and just a touch of ripe sweetness. Villa Maria is the largest privately owned vineyard in New Zealand, and its whole range is remarkably good.

🍷 Montana Riesling

🍷🍷 Villa Maria Private Bin Riesling • Stoneleigh Riesling • Montana Reserve Riesling

Sauvignon Blanc Still New Zealand's crowning glory.

Nobody else makes Sauvignon quite like this: green, gooseberryish, grassy, rich. Marlborough is still the place. Awatere Valley, close by, is also making good Sauvignon. Expect to pay $10.50–$12 for a decent bottle, generally. The Sanctuary is an excellent value at $8.50. 2000 Sauvignons are delicious, with more fruit, structure and individuality than they've had for many years.

The Sanctuary Sauvignon Blanc • Montana Sauvignon Blanc • Dashwood Sauvignon Blanc, Awatere Valley • Highfield Sauvignon Blanc, Marlborough • Oyster Bay Sauvignon Blanc, Marlborough • Villa Maria Private Bin Sauvignon Blanc • Grove Mill Sauvignon Blanc, Marlborough • Lawson's Dry Hills Sauvignon Blanc • Tohu Sauvignon Blanc, Marlborough • Villa Maria Cellar Selection Sauvignon, Marlborough • Wither Hills

Sauvignon Blanc,
Marlborough • Montana
Reserve Sauvignon
Blanc, Marlborough •
Jackson Estate
Sauvignon Blanc
♟♟♟ Hunter's Sauvignon
Blanc, Marlborough •
Villa Maria Clifford Bay
Sauvignon Blanc,
Marlborough • Villa
Maria Wairau Valley
Sauvignon Blanc

Semillon Up and coming varietal with potential—but where is all the exported wine? Most of it goes into dull Chardonnay and Sauvignon blends. Disappointing.

REDS

Cabernet Sauvignon Usually paired with Merlot to soften out its hard, minty tannins. Less fashionable than it was. Difficult to find good ripe wine to recommend under $15—this one just scrapes in at $13.50. Delegat's is one of New Zealand's biggest wine companies. They also own Oyster Bay.
♟♟ Delegat's Reserve Cabernet Sauvignon, Hawkes Bay

Merlot Previously blended with Cabernet, now more confidently made as a single varietal. More fashionable than before as Merlot is easier to ripen in unreliable climates. Single varietal Merlot is in vogue in New Zealand. These are both $13.50.

🍷🍷 Delegat's Reserve Merlot, Hawkes Bay • Montana Reserve Merlot

Pinot Noir Gamey, complex Pinot Noirs do exist, but most are lighter. Martinborough has made the breakthrough wine that everyone wants. ($25? Cheap in Côte d'Or terms). New Zealand is spending more energy than ever on its Pinot Noir project: they have discovered that Marlborough, its white wine zone, can also produce exceptional "New Zealand Red Burgundy." Its publicity machine says they are poised for world domination—another Sauvignon Blanc story. Perhaps, but it's early yet. Certainly New Zealand has more of a chance in this epic quest than rival Australia; New Zealand having the more northern-French climate.

♟♟ Wither Hills Pinot Noir
♟♟♟ Montana Marlborough Barrique Matured Pinot Noir •
Martinborough Pinot Noir

Red Blends New Zealand "claret" is becoming a popu-
lar use for lots of tricky Cabernet Sauvignon. The
Montana wine is relatively good value at $10.50.
♟♟ Montana Cabernet Sauvignon Merlot • Te Mata Estate
Cabernet Merlot
♟♟♟ Matariki Quintology, Hawkes Bay

PORTUGAL

There's a lot more to Portuguese wine than sweet, bland Mateus Rosé and dry bland Vinho Verde. There is of course Port, but that's too large a subject to venture into here. Ditto Madeira, which is undergoing a much deserved revival. Blandy's Sercial, cold from the fridge, is one of the great aperitifs of the world.

Portugal can be a maddening country, all the same. It's slow to change in many areas; old-fashioned methods and old-fashioned wines aren't necessarily a bad thing, but sometimes they result in wine that's less than fresh, under-fruited, its oak too old and tired. There's still lots of mediocre wine coming out of Portugal, though rustic, dry earthy reds can be very good with the kind of robust food the Portuguese prefer. The problem is the co-ops, who are stuck in their ways and still responsible for most of the wine-making. Historically Portugal is a *négociant* wine culture: the co-ops made huge batches of wine, the dealers blended it into the house style of their choice.

New World influences are beginning to make themselves felt, though. Why are they bothering? Partly because of the sheer scale of the potential here: Portugal has more land under vine than Australia, New Zealand and Chile combined. There are now signs of real change. Single estates are beginning to emerge. Consultants and investors are moving in. A Bordeaux winemaker has been busy in the Douro, working with Symington's Port, who have developed a red wine side to the business. Château Lafite have also bought vineyards here, as have Champagne house Roederer. José Neiva and J. P. Ramos are consultants whose names usually indicate quality. Peter Bright and David Baverstock, both Australians, are active here, and other flying winemakers are following.

Wines are generally fruitier, reds riper, whites fresher: sweet clean oak and stainless steel are making real impact.

"especially promising ... is that ... Portuguese grape varieties still rule."

What's especially promising in Portugal is that, although the usual suspects (Chardonnay, Cabernet Sauvignon) are making more headway, Portuguese grape varieties still rule. New arrivals, seeing the potential for native varietals and blends, are working to improve what's already here, which makes for a more individual menu of grapes and flavors than are to be found in most other countries. Suddenly, the world craves quirkiness, something unusual, something new. People are growing bored with the usual suspects. Portugal is well-placed to make a great success of its revitalized wine culture, though whether it is wise to focus on producing single varietals remains to be seen. (Some are too quirky for the world at large just yet. Difficult grape names don't help). In general spend as much as you can afford here—quality rises sharply after the $9 level, though there is still masses of good drinkable wine for under $8. Don't be put off by the rustic image of this country, or its sometimes chaotic wine-labeling. Remember that Australia was once considered a ridiculously unlikely country for fine wine production (and still is by much of France).

The climate isn't always kind. The Atlantic seaboard brings a cool, changeable maritime climate leaving the Portuguese producers surprisingly at the mercy of the weather. The inland zones are dramatically hotter and drier. Most good Portuguese wine is made in the northeast. The leading wine region is still the Douro (despite rivalry from other areas), in the mountain vineyards of the hilly, scenic Douro Valley.

The spare fruit from the Port industry has long been used for table wine, but now the focus is on quality and export. Port houses are getting in on the act and associating their famous names with these deliciously chunky, robust, nicely structured and elegant reds.

New Wave wines aren't always an improvement, though. There seem to be more blamelessly fruity and soft reds than there used to be; the slightly spineless

carbonic maceration effect can strip wines of too
much character. Portugal is awash with light, cherry
fruity reds that don't always match up to the vigor of
the rustic wines of old. Among the bigger, chunkier
reds there are still too many over-ripe, sweet and soupy
monsters that lack structure and tannin. Buying Portuguese wine can feel a bit like a lottery (which way
will this red wine jump?) And yet among them all
there are still bargains to be had—try Terra Boa, an
excellent $6 red.

Portugal seems like a naturally red wine zone so it's a
surprising fact that 40% of the wine made in Portugal
is white. Few were worth drinking until fairly recently,
but there's now some good, elegant wine about that
manages to keep its native accent and doesn't sell out to
the blandly international style. Little white wine is seen
outside Portugal thus far; most is still made to the tastes
of the home market.

QUALITY There are 18 DOCs, and 29 IPRs, the
next step down from DOC status. **Indicação de Prove-
nienca Regulamentada (IPR)** wines are a pretty new
thing and need time to settle down. Some mediocre
IPRs will fizzle out and disappear, and some will
become stars. A wine doesn't have to be a DOC to be
good. DOC awards can, on the contrary, be hidebound
and stultifying things. **Vinho Regional** wines, the Portuguese Vin de Pays equivalent, can be excellent. **Vinho
de Mesa**, table wine, is less reliable.

Language of the label: *Quinta* estate; *Colheita* vintage; *Maduro* old/matured; *Branco* white; *Tinto* red;

Rosado pink; *Seco* dry; *Doce, Ademado* sweet; *Reserva* aged wines; *Garrafeira* selected aged wines, should be top quality.

VINTAGES

2000 was a good year for quality, though quantity was down. Conditions were good in the southern appellations. 1995 and '92 were excellent years for longer-lived reds.

GRAPE VARIETIES

There are too many Portuguese grape varieties to list individually; Estremadura alone has 22 native grapes. Many have strictly local and limited use, and are not encountered anywhere else, like the Roupeiro, the white grape of Alentejo. Others are beginning to travel as the New Wave washes over them. The Fernão Pires, Ribatejo's staple white grape, otherwise known as Maria Gomes, is also causing excitement in Estremadura as a single varietal.

A quick grape variety tour. Up in the north in Minho, **Alvarinho** (Spain's undervalued Albariño grape) makes a few classy white wines as well as lots of dull Vinho Verde. The Douro's whites include **Gouveio** (Madeira's Verdelho, and a successful single varietal in Australia), often used in blends with **Rabigato** and **Malvasia**. The **Alicante Bouschet** is proving a good red variety in Alentejo and elsewhere, as is **Arigones**, otherwise known as **Tempranillo** (or even Tinto

Roriz). **Periquita** is one of the best and most successful of the many native reds, and is the mainstay of the southern IPRs, in Ribatejo, Estremadura and Alentejo. **Tinta Miuda** is good in Estremaduran Periquita blends. **Periquita** (aka Castelao Frances) has become an important grape variety, making light fruity wine in the southern co-ops.

Jaen, previously just used for blending, is showing it can be a superb single varietal in Beiras. The **Baga**, also from Beiras, is another rising star: traditionally thought too tannic to make as a single varietal, but becoming hugely successful as one. **Dão** reds use six local varieties, most importantly **Touriga Nacional**, the main Port grape; Touriga-Arigones blends are a mainstay of both the Dão and Douro. The Dão white grape **Encruzado** is being made as a single varietal, and there is excitement here that **Bical**, a Riesling-like grape which ages well, could really take off. **Muscat** (not Petits Grains) is even made, traditionally in Setúbal.

Of the international varietals, Chardonnay is making the most impact as a single varietal, largely because, as yet, Portuguese whites don't appear to travel well. The reds, like Cabernet Sauvignon and Merlot, are finding their niche in blending, adding polish and a degree of familiarity to native red blends.

REGIONS

ALENQUER

Hilly region to the north of Lisbon. Quinta das Setencostas ($9) is one of its best reds.
🍷 Quinta das Setencostas, Alenquer

ALENTEJO

Aka Alentejano. Scattered collection of IPRs to the
southeast of Lisbon, well inland, not far from the
Spanish border. The area includes **Reguengos IPR**.

Alentejo, previously
better known as a
cork-producer, has
been cited by many
pundits as Portu-
gal's next big thing
(Portugal's Rioja,
they say, thanks to
the use of Aragones,
aka Tempranillo). As the reputation rises, so do the
prices—these are all $11 and up. The Trincadeira
Preta, a Port grape, is used for sweet ripe savory reds.
🍷 Trincadeira, Alentejano, J. P. Ramos • Vila Santa
Alentejano • Cartuxa Evora Alentejano

BAIRRADA

North of Lisbon, south of the Douro Valley, and

adjoining Dão, Bairrada has low rolling hill country and the sort of heavy soil that makes for robust, chunky reds. Bairrada was a popular red wine zone, pre-shake-up and New Wave, and then went out of fashion—its wines seemed too rustic. Now it's on the way back. Good solid blackberry fruit from the (famously tannic) Baga grape is the secret. Good ones are spicy, savory, light but fruity, a sort of Malbec/Pinotage cross done as a Beaujolais. More often than not though Baga reds taste like a big bag of fruity goo.

🍷 Dom Ferraz Bairrada

BEIRAS

Mountainous area just beginning to produce wines for export. Some good Chardonnay is beginning to come out of Beiras. Red blends are also made, many using Touriga Nacional and Tinta Roriz (Tempranillo). Jose Neiva, one of Portugal's leading wine talents, makes the chocolate-and-cherries Jaen red and other good varietals under the Bela Fonte label.

🍷 Bela Fonte Bical • Bela Fonte, Jaen, Beiras

DÃO

Large wine region east of Bairrada, south of the Douro
Valley. This is a region of granite hills, its sporadic
vineyards appearing opportunistically in the better
spots. Portugal's best known red wines are not usually
as good as they think they are, not always as bad as we
think they are. Some are overoaked and need bottle age
to open and soften. Most are rather solid and dull,
though good ones have rich rustic fruit and herbal,
slightly earthy dryness. Wines should improve now it's
no longer mandatory for Dão wine to be made by the
co-ops.

DOURO

The great Port producing area in the north. Some of
Portugal's most exciting red wine now comes from the
Douro. Some white is made too. Many of the cheaper
reds are blamelessly but tiresomely soft and gluggy, like
a sort of Portuguese Beaujolais. The Altano wine ($9),
a bold, rich and spicy red, is from the Symington Port
family. The man behind Quinto do Crasto is Peter
Baverstock, an Aussie. It's an elegant New Wave red.
You can tell by the price tag.

🍷🍷 Altano, Symington, Douro Valley
🍷🍷🍷 Quinto do Crasto Reserva, Douro

ESTREMADURA

Very large area north of Lisbon. Thirty percent of the
local land is now under vineyard. Lots of good-value
quaffing red is made here, and quality varies. Many of
the cheapies are rough and ready: not to be excluded
entirely, but treated as carafe wines for the table.
Ramada Tinto is one such. Wines by José Neiva are
worth looking out for. Alenquer is an Estremadura
sub-region.

🍷🍷 Quinta da Pancas Cabernet Sauvignon

MINHO

Vinho Verde, meaning "green wine," is so named
because it's very fresh, young, refreshingly and pleasantly acidic. Most Vinho Verde is red. On its home turf
in the Minho region it can be terrific, very fresh, tart,
drying, exhilaratingly spritzy.

PALMELA

Lots of Periquita red is being made in this traditional
co-op-dominated southern zone, just inland of
Setúbal. Pegos Claros ($13), an elegant Periquita made
by J. P. Ramos, is still a foot-crushed wine, from a
property where Periquita is the only grape grown on
60 hectares of vines.

🍷🍷 Alianca Particular Palmela • Pegos Claros, Palmela

RIBATEJO

Ribatejo—Reds Ribatejo (aka Ribatejano) stretches northeast of Lisbon, along the Tagus river valley. Ribatejo has some progressive companies, making the sort of modern fruit-driven wines popular with export markets. Some blend local varieties like Trincadeira Preta and Periquita with new arrivals Pinot Noir and Cabernet Sauvignon. Globetrotting Peter Bright has made Fiuza an international success, though his Chardonnay is currently better than his rather soupy reds.

🍷 Terra de Lobos, Casal Branco, Ribatejo • Segado Tinto, Ribatejano

Ribatejo—Whites Massive potential here. Peter Bright's oak-aged Fiuza Chardonnay is made with malolactic fermentation and aged five months in oak. It's a weighty, buttery, figgy wine with savory yeasty oak dryness, oily preserved lemons character, spice and freshness. Fernão Pires/Chardonnay blends are also made, usually dominated by the musky spice of the native grape.

🍷 Fiuza Chardonnay

SETÚBAL

Adjoins the headland over the water from Lisbon, and is famed for its Moscatel. Some decent country red is also made.

TERRAS DO SADO

Progressive modern wine-making is just beginning to emerge here at very low prices.

🍷 Pedras do Monte, Terras de Sado

OTHER REGIONS

There are vineyard areas in the Algarve, and four DOCs, though almost all the wine is for local and tourist quaffing. There are also ancient vineyards around Lisbon, vineyards closer to the sea than any other country in the world.

Pedras do Monte

Castelão

Vinho Regional Terras do Sado

1999

Pedras do Monte is an outstanding example of "regional" wines from Terras do Sado area of Portugal's south west. The aroma and taste is of; fruits of the forest and spice. It is full bodied and rich, yet deliciously smooth. The finish is dry and very persistent.

Produce of
Portugal
Engarrafado Por:
Eng. 1207 - PT .

Para
DFJ Vinhos Lda.
2070 - 512
Portugal

12.5%vol   75cl ℮

SOUTH AFRICA

Very very little of the vast continent of Africa is suitable for cultivation of the vine. The vineyard areas are all clustered around the coastal strip of the Cape. There, despite the latitude, the maritime influences of the Atlantic and Indian Oceans and the cooler microclimates of the upland areas create a patchwork of ideal wine-growing regions.

South Africa ought to be fantastically successful as a wine country, and on the face of it, it is. It may seem mean-minded to quibble—we drink millions of bottles of the stuff, the facts speak for themselves. But . . . we don't love South African wine like we love Australian and Chilean wine. We don't respect it as much. There are reasons. The hangover of the apartheid years is certainly one factor. The fact that most South African wine is over-cropped, dilute bulk wine (75% of it white) made to a price point rather than for quality makes it difficult for the better wineries to rise above the boxed-wine image.

An astonishing 85% of South African wine is still made by the co-ops: a co-operative based wine culture doesn't make for excellence and individuality—it makes for uniformity and value. Then there is the inheritance of the plantings in the vineyards. Almost a third of South African vines grow Chenin Blanc, which in New World conditions is only rarely a quality grape. South Africa is digging up some of this stuff and planting better varieties in better vineyard sites, but so far they are just scratching the surface. More decisive action needs to be taken if South Africa wants to compete in the quality race. At the moment, trying to be both cheap and classic, Bulgaria and Bordeaux, it falls between two stools.

> "South Africa ought to be fantastically successful as a wine country..."

Having said all of that, there is lots of fantastic wine coming out of this country and some of it at least is miraculously cheap. World class $9 Shiraz isn't something you find in Australia anymore. The wine estates, over 80 of them, must by law grow their own fruit, which helps preserve the integrity and character of their wines. But nowhere is it more important to stick with good producers. The really good wineries, not all of which deal in the $15 and above market, are remarkably consistent and the name usually guarantees a good wine. Among them there is Spice Route

(now owned by Fairview), which was set up as part of
the black empowerment project, to give vineyard
workers more of a stake in their wine companies.
Other project wineries include Winds of Change,
Thandi, Fair Valley and Freedom Road.

Chenin (aided by a little Semillon) was pretty much
the only white grape variety in South Africa until relatively recently. Vines were difficult to import.
Chardonnay, Sauvignon, Riesling are all fairly new
arrivals, as are Cabernet Sauvignon, Merlot and Pinot
Noir, which have now threatened the original French
import, Cinsaut. These new plantings only really
matured in the '80s, which is one reason South African
wine has come to such prominence in the last ten
years. Sales have increased fifteenfold since 1990.
Chenin is being replaced by more interesting varieties
in many areas, notably Chardonnay and Sauvignon.
Shiraz and Merlot are the hot red grapes—particularly
Shiraz, which South Africa is discovering it can excel
at. Merlot works very well in the Cape climate, making
juicy, fruity easy wines. Pinot Noir, grown in the newer
cool zones, is beginning to cause excitement. Pinotage,
South Africa's own red grape, is still the mascot red
varietal, and deservedly so. It's good to hang on to at
least one grape variety that's not grown everywhere
else in the New World.

In general most wines are short-lived and not
intended for keeping, especially the whites, which are
best drunk young and fresh, though the bigger,
musclier Chardonnays benefit from a couple of years in
bottle. The better estates have launched some substan-

tial, longer lived reds, which have more of a bottle life. Youthful, tart reds and whites, and those whose flavors are short-lived and fade away are often just picked too early, a characteristic South African problem.

Good producers to look out for: Bellingham, Beyers Truter (Beyerskloof), Buitenverwachting, Clos Malverne, Danie de Wet (de Wetshof), Fairview, Graham Beck, Longridge (Bayview), Neil Ellis, Ryland's, Saxenburg, Spice Route, Springfield, Stellenzicht, Thandi, Thelema, Vergelegen, Villiera, Warwick, Winds of Change, Yonder Hill.

VINTAGES

The 2000 vintage was difficult as many vineyards were affected by widespread forest fires. Quantity will be down and prices will rise. Both 2000 and 1999 were hot years, early ripening. Wines will be of average quality. 1998 was also hot and perhaps lacking in acidity, though top estate Chardonnays don't reflect this. There is a consistency to the climate: wines from good producers are usually reliable. 1996 and '97 reds are drinking well now.

REGIONS

COASTAL REGION

Can mean it's from Constantia, Durbanville (fringe of Cape Town suburbs), Paarl, Stellenbosch or Tulbagh.

Given the fame of the other appellations, most likely to
be from Durbanville or Tulbagh.

CONSTANTIA

Cool coastal region close to Cape Town. Venerable,
affluent area with historic appeal: the first Cape vineyards were established here in 1685. Reds are made but
this has become a whites zone. Buitenverwachting is
the star winery.

ELGIN

The Elgin Hills separate Stellenbosch from the southeast Overburg region. A cool microclimate good for
Chardonnay; Neil Ellis's superb winery leads the (still
fairly limited) pack. Great potential here.

FRANSCHOEK

"French Corner," originally settled by Huguenots, now
a sub-region down in the southern tip of Paarl. A long,
green valley with both north-facing red grape sites,
and south-facing white grape sites. Good whites
include exciting New Wave Chenin.

HELDERBURG

Trendy hilly zone, one of the newest appellations, a
Stellenbosch sub-region. Some superb wine is coming
out of Helderburg already. Yonder Hill, who estab-

lished their vineyards here in 1989, is one of the best names to look out for. Longridge, an Australian-run and dynamic estate is here, as is Radford Dale, and Post House, a one-man winery.

ORANGE RIVER/ OLIFANTSRIVIER

Arid, hot zones in the Western Cape, redeemed by cooling Atlantic breezes and their river valley microclimate. Irrigation and high yields mean little wine is interesting; lots of bulk wine is made. Huge co-op Vredendal is here.

PAARL

Inland area, north of Stellenbosch. Previously dismissed as a fortified wine and sherry district, now making a lot of bulk wine, but also a dynamic source of good and improving wine. Fairview and Villiera are here as well as KWV. Just about every grape variety is grown in its hot valleys and cool upland slopes.

ROBERTSON

Inland area, to the east of Worcester, and across the mountains from Paarl. A hot zone with very low rainfall, but redeemed by irrigation from the Breede River, and its unusually stony, limey soils make it especially good for whites—some big rich Chardonnays are made. Danie de Wet, of de Wetshof estate, was the first to introduce cold-fermentation techniques to South Africa. Also good here: Springfield Sauvignons.

STELLENBOSCH

Just to the east of Constantia, around the bay. A varied landscape—light sandy soil in the west, granite-rich land in the east, warmer in the north, cooler on the upland sites—means all kinds of wine can be grown. Known as a premium red zone, but whites are improving as growers move off the fertile hot plains into the hills. Stellenbosch is regarded as South Africa's best wine district, not least by its own producers, and has a tendency to rest on its laurels. There is a risk here of paying for the name rather than the quality on offer. There are also quality estates like Thelema, Clos Malverne, Vergelegen and Warwick

SWARTLAND

Huge coastal headland to the north of Cape Town. Previously known as a tobacco farming area, Swartland is hot and arid, though it gets cool air off the sea. The Swartland co-op led the pack for a long time, but boutique wineries are moving in. No irrigation is used here, so fruit can be rich and concentrated. Tulbagh adjoins Swartland.

WALKER BAY

Cool upland area close to the sea and adjoining Elgin.

On the up, though output is still tiny. Hamilton Russell's Pinot Noir is currently its star wine; good Chardonnay too. Wildekrans, further inland, is becoming well known for its reds.

WORCESTER

Little known but almost 20% of the vineyards are here. Bulk wine production and a handful of good wineries. Reds are better than whites.

WESTERN CAPE

Catch-all appellation for the less famous Western Cape areas.

GRAPE VARIETIES

WHITES

Chardonnay South African Chardonnay can impress, though it rarely does so under $8. Danie de Wet's creamy, biscuity $6 wine is an exception. Generally at the cheap end there's still too much thin, weedy wine

2000

GROWN, MADE AND BOTTLED BY

DANIE DE WET

CHARDONNAY SUR LIE

UNWOODED

SOUTH AFRICA

propped up by hefty oak (or oak chips), or else overbearingly tropical, fruit salad wines full of blowsy, sickly fruit. Unwooded is sometimes best, though the yeasty, nutty, spicy, barrel-fermented style is good when it works. It's possible to find really classy Chardonnay at just $9–$11 though—try Vergelegen or Thandi, both amazingly complex and poised for the money. The Buitenverwachting wine ($13.50) is exceptional.

1998

Chardonnay

WINE OF ORIGIN CONSTANTIA

LINTON PARK • SOUTH AFRICA

CAPELL'S COURT

1999

CHARDONNAY

SOUTH AFRICA

🍷 Danie de Wet Chardonnay

🍷🍷 De Wetshof Lesca Chardonnay • Fairview Chardonnay • Thandi Chardonnay • Vergelegen Chardonnay, Stellenbosch • Call of the African Eagle Chardonnay •

Capells Court Chardonnay • Graham Beck Chardonnay •
Von Ortloff Chardonnay, Franschhoek • Warwick Estate
Chardonnay, Stellenbosch • Fairview Akkerbos
Chardonnay • Buitenverwachting Chardonnay, Constantia •
Jordan Chardonnay, Stellenbosch • Radford Dale
Chardonnay, Helderberg • Saxenburg Private Collection
Chardonnay, Stellenbosch
♟♟♟ Vergelegen Reserve Chardonnay

Chardonnay Blends These are usually cheap and not
always cheerful. Usually they are ripe, tropical and vulgar.
♟ Kumala Semillon-Chardonnay • Waterside White,
Chardonnay Colombard

Chenin Blanc (Steen) By adoption, South Africa's
national white grape variety. Chenin is the staple of
many cheap blends and box wines. As a varietal, it's
worth spending money on: the campaign to improve
Chenin's image (by first improving its flavors) is beginning to produce some exciting wine. Most of the cheap
stuff is merely crisp and blandly plump and many suf-

fer from a typical cheap-Chenin fault: oak begins to dominate the fruit half way down the glass. Good Chenin, made with care and low yields, has the capacity to age from something with earthy, fresh mown grass aromas, and a sharp, dry, green savory palate into a richer, satisfying wine, lemony and Granny Smithy, with a creamy nutty flourish. Many of the new wines, made with barrel-fermentation, have a plump and apricot-flavored, nicely textured richness, but are also good and dry. The Ryland's wine ($6) is a great bargain.

🍷 Ryland's Grove Barrel-Fermented Chenin Blanc, Kym Milne • Fair Valley Bush Vine Chenin • Fairview Barrel-Fermented Chenin Blanc

🍷🍷 Jordan Barrel-Fermented Chenin Blanc, Stellenbosch • Spice Route Chenin Blanc

Colombard Usually dull, blandly tropical, crisp vulgar whites with blowsy fruit; better ones have a dry finish and perhaps a floral note. Often blended with Chenin and Chardonnay.

Riesling Good cheap Riesling is hard to find. Some are too fruity and two-dimensional; others are just crisp and lack stuffing. Sweet dessert Rieslings are also made.

Sauvignon Blanc Good Sauvignon has been hard to find in South Africa. Often it's just too thin and weedy. Even some of the expensive stuff is pretty subtle, with a lemony, mineral accent; when these wines are also over-oaked, the result is overly drying and under-fruited. A hot-climate exotic fruit note sometimes creeps in which isn't welcome either. But Sauvignon has improved immeasurably in the last few years. Cooler growing zones and improved technique has brought lots of good wines into the shops. Some have a whiff of New Zealand about them, grassy and rich with gooseberry fruit.

> "Sauvignon has improved immeasurably … grassy and rich with gooseberry fruit."

Firefinch Sauvignon Blanc

Spice Route Sauvignon Blanc • Springfield Estate Life From Stone Sauvignon • Brampton Sauvignon Blanc • Buitenverwachting Sauvignon Blanc, Constantia • Steenberg Sauvignon Blanc • Vergelegen Reserve Sauvignon Blanc

Semillon Can be as thin and disappointing as cheap Chenin. Better ones have a fresh, grassy palate when young, acquiring more biscuity, buttery, honeyed flavors as they mature. Rarely as good as the Australian wines but Fairview's Oom Pagel ($10.50) shows the potential here.

🍷🍷 Fairview Oom Pagel Semillon

Viognier Following in the footsteps of the Australian passion for this Rhône variety. Peachy, lemon-edged, with tropical flavors, ideal for Fusion cooking. $13 seems excessive though.

🍷🍷 Fairview Viognier, Paarl

REDS

Cabernet Franc New as a single varietal for South Africa. This $8.50 wine has big juicy rich fruit like a Cape Merlot but also a Bordelais twist of tannic dryness. Could take off.

🍷🍷 Milton Grove Cabernet Franc

Cabernet Sauvignon Prices are notably higher for Cape Cabernet than for Cape Chardonnay. Little good stuff is available at $8, or even $9—Apostle's Falls ($9) is a rare exception. Generally the cheap stuff is either bland and soupy or dried out and baked-tasting. At the top end there's lots of deliciously ripe, complex wine, though some are still too jammy even at this level, and others too Bordeaux-like, being green, hard and closed, in need of some bottle age. Expect to pay $12 plus.

🍷 Oak Village Cabernet Sauvignon

ŸŸ Apostle's Falls Cabernet Sauvignon • Post House Cabernet Sauvignon, Helderberg • Saxenburg Cabernet Sauvignon, Stellenbosch • Yonder Hill Cabernet Sauvignon, Stellenbosch • Jordan Cabernet Sauvignon • Kumala Reserve Cabernet Sauvignon

ŸŸŸ Neil Ellis Cabernet Sauvignon

Cabernet Blends South African Cabernet is often better in claret-style blends, paired with Merlot (and/or Cabernet Franc). Cabernet Shiraz can also work well, the Shiraz providing a lusher foil to the dryish framework of the Cabernet fruit.

Cinsaut Masses of Cinsaut is still grown, though more international varietals are taking its place in many areas. Usually works better in blends than on its own.

Malbec Beginning to gain popularity as a single varietal. As ever Fairview shows the way with its well-
priced ($9) experimental wine. This one is rich and
ripe but has good structure.
¶¶ Fairview Malbec, Paarl

Merlot Merlot has really taken off in South Africa now,
though its easy, rich ripeness can topple over into the
merely soft and jammy. Wines can be velvet soft, and
some are sweetish. New oak makes a difference to the
structure. New Wave Merlots have rich fruit, chocolate,
raisins, tobacco-edged tannin and a hint of spice. Graham Beck's wine ($9) and Drosty-Hof's ($8.50) are
fantastic for the price.
¶¶ Drosty-Hof Merlot • Bellingham Merlot • Landskroon
Oaked Merlot Reserve • Pinnacle Merlot • Graham Beck
Merlot • Fairview Merlot • Radford Dale Merlot, Helderberg
• Yonder Hill Merlot, Helderberg

Pinot Noir Success has been very patchy, but now that
cooler climate (and especially maritime) areas are
being properly established,
South Africa is beginning to
make quality Pinot Noir.
¶¶¶ Hamilton Russel Pinot Noir,
Walker Bay

"…richly smoky
and savory, with
leathery tannins
and a
characteristic
mildly rubbery
or earthy note."

Pinotage In 1925, Pinot Noir
was crossed with Cinsaut: Pinotage is the result, and it's South
Africa's national red. Some

cheaper Pinotages can merely be mildly smoky and savory, putting the emphasis firmly on ripe strawberry fruit. More interesting wines reveal themselves in layers of flavor, richly smoky and savory, with leathery tannins and a characteristic mildly rubbery or earthy note.

🍷 Rock Ridge Pinotage
🍷🍷 Bellingham Pinotage •
Beyerskloof Pinotage, Stellenbosch • Neil Joubert Pinotage • Clos Malverne Pinotage • Fairview Pinotage

Shiraz Originally used in blending, South African Shiraz (Syrah) has traditionally been more restrained, more red berryish and softly spicy than, say, the big blackcurrant monsters of Australia, though some at the top end tended to be rather port-like, alcoholic and solid. Shiraz is now finding its niche as a single varietal and has become hugely trendy. The New Wave wine is taking on the Australian model and creating its

> "There's lots of designer wine at $15 and above—
> …but not all of this is convincing for the money."

own style, rich, peppery and well-structured, for those international, Shiraz-hungry markets. These first three listings are all $10.50 and under: the Porcupine Ridge wine is particularly good. Generally good wine is $13.50 and above. There's lots of designer wine at $15 and above—some $30 and above—but not all of this is convincing for the money. Australia, and yes even the Rhône have more structure and elegance and quirky individuality in the super-league. So far.

🍷🍷 Porcupine Ridge Shiraz • Fairview Shiraz • Bellingham Shiraz • Graham Beck Shiraz, Coastal Region • Fairview Reserve Shiraz

🍷🍷🍷 Radford Dale Shiraz, Helderberg • Graham Beck The Ridge Shiraz

Red Blends South Africa excels here. Like Australia, New World "claret" is made with Cabernet and Merlot (like the delicious Spice Route wine, which has fruit Bordeaux would kill for), but also iconoclastic Bordeaux-Rhône mixes of Cabernet and Shiraz.

🍷 Bouwland Cabernet Sauvignon Merlot, Stellenbosch • Kumala Cabernet Sauvignon Shiraz • Railroad Cabernet Sauvignon Shiraz • Winds of Change Pinotage Cabernet Sauvignon

🍷🍷 Fairview Zinfandel Cinsault • Spice Route Andrew's Hope Cabernet Merlot • Yonder Hill Inanda

SPAIN

We're ambivalent about Spain. There's lots of gorgeous wine at fairly bargain prices to be had here but many of us would prefer to risk a French bottle or something safe from the New World. Partly this is down to image. In total contrast to Italy, Spain is downmarket in our imaginations. Spain is a rustic country and a bit vulgar—we think—as if the wine is tainted by our visions of bullfights and sad donkeys and Benidorm and all-day breakfasts washed down with lager. It's also partly down to reliability. Or lack of. Whereas we feel confident about lifting a bottle marked Produce of Australia or Produce of Chile, the Spanish bottle is more of an unknown quantity. It hasn't New World consistency of excellence stamped all over it. Neither is it likely to be Cabernet Sauvignon, Merlot, Chardonnay or Sauvignon (although it might be, the way things are going), grapes we feel we know and can trust.

The rather 1970s image of well-known brands like Rioja doesn't help. Without tasting around the country widely, with an open mind, it's easy to think that all good quality Spanish red has that familiar Rioja shape and flavor—rich dark plum and strawberry, vanilla oak, tannin, alcohol, wham. Rioja can seem dull and old-fashioned. And a lot of it is, actually. But there is also New World influence even here, in the most traditional of regions. And masses of New Wave activity all over this big wine country, producing superb, elegant, modern reds and delicious modern whites that will knock your socks off. So banish those prejudices and give it a go.

Spain is having a bit of a crisis just presently. Grape prices collapsed in 2000. Yields are ridiculously high—too much wine is being made, and some of that is unacceptably dull and dilute. In Rioja they got greedy after world interest revived in them—the fashion for neighboring appellations rubbed off on them a little—and subsequently increased their production by almost 50%, even planting vineyards on farmland down on the plain, where quality had to suffer. Over-production is a national problem, but the good estates and the forward-looking producers are going the other way, looking to quality, to low yields and wines with individuality. Successful neighbors like Ribera del Duero and Navarra are frankly a bit embarrassed by Rioja.

The New Wave is now making a real impact in

Spain but this doesn't have the publicity it deserves. In the spirit of experimentation, some vineyards are daring to use "unauthorized" grape varieties, accepting that the resulting wine will have to be labeled Vino de Mesa, like Marqués de Griñón's fabulous Syrah. In general the radicals are getting away from prolonged oak aging, and even some traditionalists are following.

There is a widespread recognition that wines can get old and tired hanging about in barrels too long, and that the big wide world craves FRUIT.

> "wines can get old and tired hanging about in barrels too long, and ... the world craves FRUIT."

Spain has the largest vineyard acreage in the world, and is the world's third largest producer, after Italy and France. But it has been slow to develop its quality table wine, other than for Rioja. Like its neighbor Portugal, Spain has always been dominated by its fortified wine tradition; it allowed sherry to define its relationship with the world. Table wines were rustic, rough, for drinking at home. The exception was Rioja, just over the Pyrenees from France, whose style was shaped by the demands and tastes of Bordeaux during the devastation of its own vineyards by phylloxera. Other regions in the northeast simply followed in Rioja's path.

French grape varieties have now arrived in numbers and are being made as single varietals, particularly Chardonnay. Cheeringly, they are often at their most interesting when teamed up with native grape varieties, perhaps blending Chardonnay with Viura, or Cabernet Sauvignon with Tempranillo and Garnacha. Some native varieties are also proving to be good as single varietals. There's huge potential. Spain is now capable of making outstanding Cabernet and Syrah, Chardonnay and Sauvignon. Its trump card is that it is also beginning to produce outstanding single varietal Tempranillo, Garnacha and Albariño. Not always with hefty oak, either.

QUALITY:

DO Like a French AC or an Italian DOC.

DOC The new, higher quality band, so far only applicable to Rioja. The DOC label is fairly meaningless.

Vino de Mesa Table wine. Usually cheap and none too cheerful. In a few cases it's found on the labels of exciting New Wave wines denied DO status.

Crianza At least a year in wood, followed by bottle aging. Not released for sale until its third birthday.

Reserva Wine judged to be of good quality given at least three years to mature (two for whites). At least a year is spent in wood (six months for whites). Not released for five years.

Gran Reserva Wine judged—by their producers—to be of superior quality, given two years at least in wood and three in bottle (or the reverse). Not released for six years. Whites spend six months in wood and four years altogether.

Language of the label: *Cosecha* vintage; *Criado y Embotellado* grown and bottled; *Elaborado y Anejado* made and aged; *Blanco* white; *Tinto* red; *Rosado* pink; *Seco* dry; *Dulce* sweet.

VINTAGES

2000 was beset by heat and drought. It will be a good year for Rioja and for Ribera del Duero. In general vintages vary from region to region, as the climates of Spain are so diverse. 1993–5 were short years owing to adverse weather; 1993 was the worst year in recent memory. 1995 and '96 were good quality everywhere, as were '88–'90. 1999 was especially good in Rioja.

GRAPE VARIETIES

WHITES

Airén Few have heard of it, but this is the most planted white grape variety in the world. A huge acreage grows in the hot center of Spain. Traditionally, a strongly alcoholic, rough white, it can be light, crisp and spicy in the right hands.

Albariño Apricot, lemon and soft alcohol feature in the New Wave Albariños. Spain's most exciting white grape variety.

Chardonnay Taking root in the newer cool climate vineyards. Tends to be yeasty and waxy, with peach, lemon and oak, and not in the crisp lean style.
🍷 Jaume Serra Chardonnay
🍷🍷 Castillo de Molina Chardonnay Reserve

Garnacha Blanca White Grenache. Used in some white blends.

Malvasia Behind many of Spain's old-fashioned whites: plump, full-flavored, yellowish, low in acidity and freshness. Well-grown and made, can be an intriguing, tasty grape variety, with peachy, nutty character.

Moscatel Best known for (Muscat of Alexandria) dessert wines in Valencia. This is also the fresh, appley, floral grape of Viña Esmeralda.

Parellada Bulk white grape used in the northeast and for Cava. At its best in Viña Sol.

Sauvignon Blanc Can be surprisingly good, especially from the cool hillside slopes of the northeast.

Verdejo The reason Marqués de Riscal went to Rueda. Plump, creamy, nutty, but also fresh and dry. As

Verdelho, this is now a hit grape variety in Western Australia.

Viura Also known as Maccabeo. Can be excitingly complex and aromatic in the hands of a good producer. Good with Chardonnay. The main white Rioja grape.

REDS

Bobal Used in many of the lighter reds of the south.

Cabernet Sauvignon Now beginning to show its potential in Spain. Many are still rather solid and over-oaked, with hefty tannins, but the trend is towards fresher and more elegant wines.

Cariñena Carignan, also known as Mazuelo. Robust tannins and acids mean it ages well in good red blends. Used in some Riojas.

Garnacha Grenache. A huge acreage is grown here, mostly for blends, though good single varietal Garnacha is increasingly popular.

Graciano Rare but fine quality Rioja grape.

Mazuelo *see* **Cariñena**

Monastrell Often used with Tempranillo, and to bulk

out lots of dreary east coast reds. But finding a new lease on life in New Wave hands. Good with Cabernet and Merlot.

Tempranillo Also known as Cencibel, Tinto de Toro, or just Tinto. Spain's star red grape variety, widely used in quality blends in Rioja and Navarra, and all over the place. Can excel as a single varietal: the juicy, fresh modern style is often available at very low prices.

🍷 Modernista Tempranillo • Tierra Sana Organic Tempranillo • Alteza 750 Tempranillo • Espiral Tempranillo Cabernet

WINE REGIONS

Calatayud An Aragon DO, traditionally the source of budget country reds, but now looking more modern. Ditto sister appellation Campo de Borja. These two delicious country wines are both sub-$6.

🍷 Gran Lopez Tinto, Campo de Borja • Viña Fuerte Garnacha

Conca de Barbera Catalonian DO. A rather hit and miss appellation. Torres Chardonnay is good.

Costers del Segre A Catalonian DO to the south of Penedès. Costers del Segre and Raimat are almost one and the same thing. Certainly Raimat is the only winery of note. Wines are $10.50 plus.

🍷🍷 Raimat Cabernet Sauvignon • Raimat Tempranillo • Raimat Merlot

Jumilla Jumilla is to the east of Valdepeñas, just west of Alicante. Part of the huge vineyard area known as the Levante, along with Valencia and Utiel Requena. It's very hot, and the tradition here is for big, alcoholic, almost sherry-like sturdy reds, but there's now lots of fruitier fresher wine about at bargain prices. Look out for the superb Taja range, owned and run by winemakers from Bordeaux. They use Cabernet Sauvignon and Merlot in their Tempranillo blends. The Gran Reserva is $11.

♀ Taja Tinto, Jumilla • Taja Reserva, Jumilla

♀♀ Taja Gran Reserva, Jumilla

La Mancha south of Madrid is a huge plain of endless vineyards where almost half Spain's wine is grown. Valdepeñas is a Mancha sub-region. Lots of Airén, Tempranillo and Garnacha here. Most La Mancha wine is pretty dreadful, but some modern Valdepeñas reds are pretty good, soft and richly fruity. If a very cheap supermarket Spanish wine has no other distinguishing marks, it's probably from La Mancha.

Navarra Navarra is in the north, next to Rioja. Traditionally these were Garnacha (Grenache) vineyards, lots of their fruit used for rosado, but more and more Tempranillo is being used, often in Garnacha blends. Cabernet Sauvignon and Merlot are being planted in quantity and appear both in blends and as single varietals. Navarra is now one of the best appellations in Spain for good medium-priced red, as well as surprisingly good Chardonnay (if you can find it). Wines from Julian Chivite are always reliable, and Agramont is a pretty decent name when on form. Look out for Guelbenzu.

🍷 Ochoa Tempranillo Garnacha
🍷🍷 Palacio de la Vega Cabernet Tempranillo Crianza •
Chivite Gran Feudo Reserva, Navarra

Penedes In Catalonia, just outside Barcelona. Torres is the most important winery here. Miguel Torres was instrumental in the rebirth of Spanish wine, not least by introducing French varietals some 40 years ago. Some of their white is made in nearby Conca de Barbera. The deliciously fresh, floral, Granny Smith-flavored Viña Esmeralda is 85% Moscatel, 15% Gewürztraminer,

and cold-fermented in stainless steel. Viña Sol is 100% Parellada. Cool-climate zones up here in the shade of the Pyrenees mean there's lots more potential for good white varietals. Penedès is also the home of Cava (*see* FIZZ).

🍷 Torres Viña Sol
🍷🍷 Torres Viña Esmeralda • Torres Gran Viña Sol • Torres

Atrium Merlot • Torres Gran Sangre de Toro • Torres Gran Coronas Reserva

Priorato Most celebrated (trendy) of the Catalonian DOs, known for its monster reds, elegant and long-lived. No bargains.
🍷🍷🍷 Mas Igneus FA206

Rias Baixas is up in the far north west in Galicia, a white wine zone. Traditionally, wines are light, dry, made for fish and seafood. The New Wave is beginning to turn out richer, quirkier wines, which are now becoming fashionable—snap them up if you can find them. Lagar de Cervera wines are interesting if pricey—dry, savory, quinine-tinged and robust. They make a good alternative to fino sherry as an aperitif.
🍷🍷 Albariño Condes del Alberei • Albariño Pazo de Seoane

Ribera del Duero is in the central north, with Navarra and Rioja as its appellation neighbors. The Duero valley extends west into Portugal, where the river becomes the Douro of Port wine fame. A hot inland zone (though blessed with cool nights and chalky soils) traditionally dedicated to sturdy, alcoholic reds, has now been reborn as the deeply fashionable Ribera del Duero. Bordeaux is a major influence here: Vega Sicilia, the top wine, uses mostly claret grapes. Prices are fairly high and there are few bargains: wines start at about $15. Pesquera is the current darling. Look out for Abadia Retuerta, on the fringes of the appellation. This Rivola is a Ribera bargain at $11.

♟♟ Abadia Retuerta Rivola
♟♟♟ Pago de Carraovejas • Pesquera Reserva Tinto

Rioja Twenty percent of the red Spanish wine sold in Britain is Rioja. This is mostly an upland area, in which the heat of the Spanish summer is tempered by a long growing season and plenty of rain. Rioja Alta is the coolest zone, producing fruit that has good acids and structure: some of the best, longest lived wines come from here, and some of the most innovative producers. Rioja Alavesa fruit is generally softer, easier, more aromatic, but has a shorter lifespan. Rioja Baja wines are considered the coarsest of the three: they're Garnacha-based, in the hottest district, and are grown on heavier soils.

It's unusual for single estate wines to be made; most blend wines—even using some from other Rioja regions—to achieve their own house style. The traditional grape varieties are Tempranillo, Garnacha, Graciano and/or Mazuelo, but 100% Tempranillo wines are now also made and it's becoming fashionable to make Tempranillo/Cabernet Sauvignon blends. Barrel aging is customary: wines soften out and acquire sweet vanilla oak. Lengthy barrel aging is gradually being replaced by earlier bottling, for better, fresher fruit. Tank fermentation is also catching on—Reservas might spend a year in tank before transferring to American oak. Unoaked, or briefly oaked wines, now among Rioja's most popular, are labeled sin *crianza* (or *joven*). *Crianza* wines are aged for up to a year only. The best recent Rioja years were '99 and '95, the worst '93 and '97.

🍷 Rioja Joven Viña Arisabel • Siglo 1881 Rioja

🍷🍷 Artadi Orobio Rioja • Marqués de Griñón Rioja • Viña Mara Rioja • Cosme Palacio y Hermanos Rioja • Campo Viejo Reserva Rioja • Gran Condal Rioja Reserva • Viña Herminia Graciano Reserva Rioja

🍷🍷🍷 Marqués de Riscal Rioja Reserva

Rioja—White Viura, Malvasia, and perhaps also white Garnacha are used in the blends. Traditionally the whites, too, got a hefty dose of oak aging—perhaps four or five years in barrel, till they were densely golden and had strong flavors. Some of these old-fashioned wines still exist, but the trend now is for much lighter, fruitier wines with more Viura in the blend. This can mean whites that are too blandly fruity, however. The famous Marqués de Murrieta is of the old school, an oak aged Malvasia-based wine: peachy in color, sherryish in flavor with dramatic fruit and lemon attack on the tastebuds and drying, chewy oak.

♟♟ Cosme Palacio y Hermanos • Dominio de Montalvo • Muga Rioja Blanco • Marqués de Murrieta
♟♟♟ Conde de Valdemar Barrique Fermented Rioja

Rosado Not a region, but the Spanish word for pink wine. Both Navarra and Rioja are turning out some delicious, full-bodied but crisp rosado, gorgeous for summer but with enough oomph for food.

♟ Chivite Gran Feudo Rosado, Navarra
♟♟ Marqués de Carceres Rosado, Rioja

Rueda Marqués de Riscal were responsible for sparking the big changes now underway in Rueda: they were looking for a cooler climate zone and settled here, close to Ribera del Duero. The local grape variety, Verdejo, was also an attraction. This is potentially a cracking white region. The oxidized sherryish whites of yesteryear are being ousted in favor of modern fruit-driven wines, even some Sauvignon Blanc. Some Rueda Blancos are still barrel-aged for a honeysuckle and peaches-in-liqueur character with lots of alcohol and oak (try Marqués de Riscal): others are crisp and steely, too crisp and steely on occasion. The Sauvignon style is mild, soft and gooseberryish. Cheap modern wines from Viños Sanz are okay, a little dull.

Somontano A fairly new Aragón appellation, enjoying
a cool microclimate in the foothills of the Pyrenees.
Somontano is proving good for Chardonnay and for
Pinot Noir, as well as the more traditional varieties.
Spain tastes most New World in Somontano but wines
still have a pronounced Spanish accent.

🍷 Viñas del Vero Chardonnay

🍷🍷 Viñas del Vero
Merlot • Viñas del Vero
Cabernet Sauvignon •
Enate Cabernet Merlot
• Enate Crianza
Tempranillo Cabernet
Sauvignon

Tarragonna A Catalonian DO, gaining a reputation for
its Garnacha reds. Cellers de Capçanes is the top estate,
its excellent Mas Collet red ($9) a Cabernet-Spanish
blend. The Costers del Gravet wine is $13. Look out
too for wines from the neighboring Terra Alta DO.

🍷 Mas Donis Capçanes

🍷🍷 Mas Collet Capçanes • Costers del Gravet Capçanes

Toledo Spain now has its own equivalent of the Italian
Super-Tuscan in the quite extraordinary reds of Marqués de Griñón, completely outside the regulations
and thus condemned to mere Vino de Mesa status.
Prices have risen but so has the quality—these wines
are of a standard to make even Australians gnash their
teeth. The Syrah is Spain's first.

🍷🍷🍷 Marqués de Griñón Dominio de Valdepusa Cabernet

Sauvignon • Marqués de Griñón
Dominio de Valdepusa Syrah

Utiel Requena is a baking hot region in inland Valencia, just to the east of La Mancha. Efforts are being made to overhaul its traditionally baked, soupy, dry reds and some good simple

> "...these wines are of a standard to make even Australians gnash their teeth."

fruity stuff is emerging, as well as Maccabeo-based summer quaffing whites. This New Wave red ($13.50) is in another league however.

🍷🍷 Ceremonia, Utiel Requina

Valdepeñas A sub-region in the south of La Mancha, Valdepeñas reds are a mix of red and white grape varieties, blending Airén with Tempranillo. The Viña Albali winery makes decent cheapies.

Valencia churns out lots of dreary Levante red, but is perhaps better known for its Moscatels, intensely sweet dessert wines at low prices. The best have freshness and bite to counter the stickiness. Gandia is the top producer.

Yecla Neighbor of Jumilla. Its traditional Monastrell reds are being reworked for international tastes. Try this juicy food red for around $7.

🍷 Bodegas Castano Monastrell Merlot

UNITED STATES OF AMERICA
(CALIFORNIA)

Question. What has happened to Oregon and Washington State? The last edition of the guide was full of praise for their Pinot Noirs and Cabernet Sauvignons respectively. But very little appears to be available on the British High Street from either these days. Retailers' lists are moving their American sections from the back (U for USA) to near the front of the catalogue, under C for California. USA and California are pretty much interchangeable now it seems.

California wine is both a triumph and a disaster. A triumph because its very best Pinot Noirs and Chardonnays are fabulous things, chased by collectors the world over. A disaster in several ways: for one, because lots of the expensive wine (and most California wine is expensive) is just laughably bad—juicy ripe stuff that just isn't worth the $21 or whatever price they're asking. Masses of sweet fruit and a forest-load of oak isn't always enough. Also disastrous, the quality of lots of the medium-priced and cheap stuff, which, sorry, just can't come close to the quality of $9–$15 wine from Chile, Australia or south of France. Time after time an opened bottle delivers fruit beaten into a corner by massively overbearing oak dryness, or else, more commonly, ripe, juicy sweet (too sweet) fruit without enough tannin and structure to support it. The Gallo range is a prime example—the wines tasted pretty good four years ago, mass-market but pretty good, and they are amazingly successful as a brand, but, frankly, it has to be said, they are just great bottles of soupy ripe goo. (Is glossy magazine advertising about Grandpa Gallo coming to America to start a vineyard enough? Evidently so.) Californians are terribly serious-minded. California winemakers take themselves terribly seriously. They sometimes seem to regard a groovy vineyard name or a well-known consultant or just the magic words Napa Valley as a passport to riches, quality in the bottle notwithstanding.

"California wine is both a triumph and a disaster."

Having said all of which, there are optimistic signs at the cheap end. Budget Californian would have been a total no-no five years ago, but there are wines listed below with $8 or $9 price-tags attached that offer something really delicious and good. You have to kiss an awful lot of frogs before you find your prince though.

Local shortages, spiraling demand and in some cases shameless greed have all led to hefty price rises. Californians are adept at believing their own publicity and there are plenty of collectors out there prepared to pay top dollar for the fashionable labels. Most good California wine is intercepted long before it can get exported, particularly if it's Pinot Noir, which has cult appeal. Prices are still ascending, though some producers, to their credit, have set their sights at quality mid-priced wine. Fetzer are still the beacon on common sense at the $9–$12 level, making a range of wines

pretty consistent in their quality and popular appeal. They are a forward-looking company, growing much of their fruit organically (Bonterra is the totally organic range). Their 720 acre property was a working ranch when the Fetzer family bought it in 1958.

Work is still being done in California to find the right sites. *Terroir* is becoming increasingly important in American wine-making, particularly in the complex geography and microclimates of California. Certain specialties are emerging: Russian River Valley is known for Pinot Noir, Alexander Valley for Cabernet Sauvignon, while Santa Barbara, also good for Pinot Noir, is fast becoming a Syrah zone.

Chardonnay is the most grown American grape, followed by Colombard, Cabernet Sauvignon and Zinfandel. There is lots of optimism about the Rhône reds, Syrah and Grenache, which may yet turn out to be more suitable grapes than the Bordeaux varieties for these climates and terrain. Syrah is now hugely popular, and Italian varieties are much in vogue, too. Viognier also does well, as do dessert wines and fizz.

In general California wine should be drunk young and fresh. Wines tire and disintegrate after a few years—1996 wines are collapsing now, though better quality Cabernet Sauvignons, Malbecs and Pinot Noirs are still drinking well. Good reds can take a decade in bottle if they are really special. Whites seem to peak at about two years old and then tail off.

VINTAGES

2000 was mostly very good, though late-picked Cabernet Sauvignon, Merlot and Zinfandel suffered from stormy harvest conditions. Whites and Pinot Noir should be better: this will be a good Chardonnay year. 1999 was small but good, '98 very patchy, '97 excellent, '96 small but good, '95 okay, better for reds, as was '94. 1993 was a better white year, '92 okay, '91 good for reds, and '90 an all-around classic.

REGIONS

CALIFORNIA

AVAs, Approved Viticultural Areas are about geography, not quality. There are 70 AVAs in California alone.

California makes 90% of American wine. The soil, rocks, sites, grapes, weather conditions, slopes, openness to cool Pacific air (in short, the *terroir*)—all these mean that it's difficult to pinpoint distinct regional styles, and this is even true within the individual wine districts.

North of San Francisco Bay, there's: **Sonoma** (coastal, but protected by an intermediary mountain range); **Napa Valley**, inland, to Sonoma's east; **Mendocino**, the northernmost California region, and **Carneros**, a cool microclimate zone to the south of Napa.

Carneros, a fairly new wine district, straddles both Sonoma and Napa. It's cooled by Bay air and thus is a natural for Chardonnay and Pinot Noir. Russian River Valley, good for Pinot Noir, is another cool Sonoma area. Sonoma Chardonnay is as good as Napa's, and good Cabernet Sauvignon also comes from here.

Napa Valley is the nerve center of California wine. It's 20 miles long and yet has three climate zones within it. Cooler in the south, hotter in the north, Napa has the most ideal conditions for wine-growing in all America.

Mendocino is drier and hotter than it looks from the map. High mountains keep its valleys warm, though it also has cool microclimate zones, like Anderson Valley. Up and coming appellation **Lake County** is proving good for Sauvignon.

South of San Francisco Bay is the **South Bay** area. The northern section is taken up by **Santa Cruz**, the southern by **Monterey**. Monterey can turn out good Pinot Noir, as well as Chenin, Riesling, and some Cabernet.

The Central Coast, a huge area leading south again from Monterey, runs through San Luis and Edna Valley into **Santa Barbara** and **Santa Ynez** valley. These are relatively cool areas with a great future. **Temecula** is down south towards San Diego.

Inland, behind the huge mountain ranges, is a huge area called **Central Valley** (aka San Joaquin). Eighty percent of California wine is made here on great flat open acreages of vines, in hot conditions needing irrigation water. Only a third of the crop is used for wine; California raisins account for much of the remainder. Grapes become sweet and dilute in the very hot, highly irrigated conditions. Lots of bulk white blends and box wine are made. This is also the home of **Gallo**, the biggest winery in the world. Astonishingly Gallo makes more wine than THE WHOLE OF AUSTRALIA.

"Astonishingly Gallo makes more wine than THE WHOLE OF AUSTRALIA."

GRAPE VARIETIES

WHITES

Chardonnay Masses of new planting is being done in the cooler zones—lots of the existing vineyards are in too warm a spot. California Chardonnay used to be a big oaky affair, though it prided itself on having a more European feel than, say, the big oaky, fruity monsters of Australia. Over-oaking is now much less common, except at the very top end, where it's still considered the thing to do. Good California Chardonnay is ripe but elegant; the best are wonderfully seamless, unwrapping in the mouth into something at once fruity, creamy, delicately tart and dry. Many of the cheaper wines are sweet and creamy, or else bold and tropical, like Fetzer's Sundial. Corbett Canyon, at just $7, is a big fruity alcoholic bruiser. Jekel Chardonnay is creamy and rich: good value at $12. The Landmark wine, though expensive, is a benchmark Chardonnay of its type—elegant, complex, Burgundian in style. Acacia tastes as though it's modeled itself on Landmark.

🍷 Corbett Canyon Chardonnay • Pacific Coast Chardonnay, Kym Milne • Stonybrook Chardonnay

🍷🍷 Fetzer Sundial Chardonnay • Mandolin Chardonnay • Talus Chardonnay • Dunnewood Chardonnay • Jekel Gravelstone Chardonnay • Mondavi Coastal Chardonnay • Wente Riva Ranch Chardonnay

¶¶¶ Acacia Chardonnay, Carneros • Landmark Overlook Chardonnay, Sonoma

Chardonnay Blends Chenin and Semillon are commonly mixed in with Chardonnay and can make good budget white. Walkers Pass is a miraculously good estate for the price. Their blend uses 30 year old Monterey Chenin vines. Ironstone is also a good reliable estate to look out for, with good wine across their range.

¶ Walkers Pass Old Vine Chenin Chardonnay
¶¶ Ironstone Semillon Chardonnay

Chenin Used mostly for cheap white blends, usually with Colombard. Cold-fermented single varietals can be quite good, sharp and fresh.

Colombard Used mostly for cheap white blends, with Chenin.

Muscat Muscat isn't a grape that springs to mind in California, but Andrew Quady in the Central Valley has made a good and unusual sticky from the rare

Orange Muscat grape variety, with orange and mango flavors and a peaches-in-brandy, marmalade character. Fetzer's wine is on more familiar territory, honeyed and peachy, unctuous but also fresh.

🍷🍷 Essensia Orange Muscat • Fetzer Bonterra Late Harvest Muscat, Mendocino

Riesling Difficult to grow here without sacrificing its complexity and piercing acidity. California Rieslings are usually plump and dreary. Very out of fashion and widely discontinued, other than for sweet late harvest wines.

> "California Rieslings are usually plump and dreary ..."

Sauvignon Blanc Good Sauvignon sites are still being developed, and there's not much good stuff about as yet. Whether California Sauvignon is going to be able to compete internationally remains to be seen: too many at present are either bland or overly tropical and ripe. Beringer, a good estate in general, makes subtle benchmark Sauvignons in the mid-price range; the Fumé Blanc is an oaked style.

🍷 Fetzer Echo Ridge Sauvignon Blanc
🍷🍷 Beringer Sauvignon Blanc • Beringer Fumé Blanc, Napa Valley

Semillon Some good varietal Semillon is made, though its main role is to add a little something to Sauvignon.

Viognier Viognier is increasingly trendy. Fetzer's wine has pears, honeysuckle, lime and peach.

🍷🍷 Fetzer Echo Ridge Viognier

🍷🍷🍷 Fetzer Bonterra Organic Viognier

REDS

Cabernet Sauvignon California is capable of world class Cabernet. Unfortunately you generally have to pay through the nose for it. Snob value for certain vineyards has pushed prices sky high, and a lot of this top end wine is almost too rich and intense to drink. Medium priced stuff is erratic and very vintage dependent. Good stuff is ripe and round, complex and softly dry, with tannins well in check, though in Napa Valley they make a more classically tannic style. Most wine is around and over the $15 level.

🍷🍷 Fetzer Valley Oaks Cabernet Sauvignon • Beringer Cabernet Sauvignon • Seven Peaks Cabernet Sauvignon

Grenache California is busy developing the Rhône Ranger reds and is beginning to have some success with single varietals. Syrah is the more fashionable grape, but a lot more Grenache than Syrah is grown. It tends to be light-bodied and pronouncedly alcoholic, though. Pinks are also made from the red Grenache grape, though confusingly they are referred to as White Grenache.

Malbec Generally used for blending in expensive, highly-wrought Bordeaux-style reds but occasionally pops up as a single varietal.
♟♟♟ Edgewood Estate Napa Valley Malbec

Merlot Deeply trendy in America and really taking off in California, though this is still a Washington speciality. Prices can be too high for the juicy, ripe style of wine on offer, though some wines go for the blockbuster, monster-Merlot approach, which generally doesn't work either. Many wines still fall short of New World standards.
♟♟ Eagle Peak Merlot, Fetzer • Ironstone Vineyards Merlot, Kautz • Bonterra Organic Merlot, Fetzer • Mondavi Coastal Merlot

Petit Verdot Like Malbec, usually a blending wine used in "California Claret," but good, if pricey, single varietals are now also made.
♟♟ Yorkville Petit Verdot, Mendocino

Petite Syrah Not to be confused with Syrah proper. Despite the fluffy name, a rather austere, dry grape variety, usually best in blends with more generously fruity grapes.

Pinot Noir The quality of its Pinot Noir lies at the heart of California's reputation. California "Red Burgundy" is the best outside France—many regard it as the equal of the Côte d'Or, or even . . . (perish the thought). Export markets wait with open checkbooks. Those that fall short of the sublime Burgundian standard may just be soft, raspberry fruity, delicately earthy, though some are surprisingly rich, deep and ripe. Prices can be silly for the fashionable wineries. Sterling Vineyards' Redwood Trail wine ($10) is generally excellent value though recent vintages have been disappointing.

🍷🍷 Redwood Trail Pinot Noir • Mondavi Coastal Pinot Noir

🍷🍷🍷 Sanford Pinot Noir

Syrah Could be California's Next Big Thing as many producers realize that Rhône varietals work better than Bordeaux grapes in their vineyard conditions. Lots is being planted. Wines coming through are good value and show real conviction.

🍷🍷 Ironstone Vineyards Shiraz, Kautz • Fetzer Syrah, Mendocino

Zinfandel California's most characteristic grape variety, grown everywhere by almost everyone. Good ones are richly red-berryish and chunky, with robust food-friendly tannins and acids. Some have a creamy texture which contrasts well with the fresh dark fruit. Walkers Pass shows ripe and brambly California Zin is possible at just $8. The Four Vines wine is twice the price but is a class act, with its lush fruit, blackcurrants and exotic notes, supported by good tannins. Some wines are

becoming too alcoholic (16% plus).

🍷 Walkers Pass Old Vine Zinfandel

🍷🍷 Beringer Zinfandel Blush • Fetzer Valley Oaks Zinfandel • Firestone Old Vine Cucmunga Zinfandel • Fetzer Bonterra Zinfandel, Mendocino

🍷🍷🍷 Four Vines Zinfandel • Ravenswood Zinfandel, Napa

REST OF THE WORLD

AUSTRIA

Austria is finally recovering from the anti-freeze scandal of 1985 and is finding its niche in the world marketplace. Some decent red and crisp flavorsome white is beginning to emerge at last, though Austrian wine will always be a minority interest. After a major flirtation with French varietals, particularly Cabernet Sauvignon (and some Merlot), many Austrian producers are turning to their native grapes once again and looking to improve vineyard sites and technique. The introduction of irrigation in some locations has made a big difference to the quality of the fruit. Some good Beerenauslese sweet wine is also made here. Wines from Lenz Moser are the most reliable.

Grüner Veltliner is the national white varietal: dry,

fairly acidic, with grapefruit, quinine, herbal and bayleaf flavors. Quality Grüner Veltliner can age well and develop a richer palate. Riesling, Sauvignon, Pinot Blanc (Weissburgunder) and Pinot Gris (Grauburgunder) are also grown. Austrians prefer their white wines tart and young.

"Austria is finally recovering from the anti-freeze scandal of 1985 and is finding its niche in the world marketplace."

Blauer Zweigelt is Austria's most characteristic red, Beaujolais-like in its soft, slightly bubblegummy palate, jammy and a little earthy. Blaufrankisch is sturdy and chunky, an Austrian Cabernet. Pinot Noir has been long established in Austria but wines tend to be simple and cherryish.

BULGARIA

Bulgaria has been relegated into Rest of The World from a main entry in the last edition because the quality of Bulgarian wine is nose-diving and there isn't much to recommend. Bulgaria's heyday seems to have come and gone. A few years ago there were lots of pleasantly rustic country reds and fresh simple whites around. Now too many reds seem either juicy gloop or dry and earthy, too many whites dull and blandly tropical.

Other countries, even France, are producing $6 wine with better fruit and more style, so why risk disappointment here?

There is the promise of improvement. Bulgaria is apparently going through a blip, waiting for land reform and vineyard investment to take effect. Maybe. Time will tell.

Meanwhile, if $5 is all that can be afforded, there are still some decent Bulgarians on offer. But watch out—words like Premium are pretty loosely applied. There are "premium" wines around that are distinctly mediocre.

Controliran is Bulgaria's version of Appellation Contrôlée, used mainly for single varieties from select regions. Below it on the quality scale is Country Wine, which is always a blend of two grape varieties. Réserve wines have lingered in barrel for a minimum two years, or up to four. Special Réserve is only applied to limited parcels, often but not always Controliran.

GRAPE VARIETIES

Bulgaria made a decision to plant masses of Chardonnay, Sauvignon, Cabernet Sauvignon and Merlot, but often their own grape varieties make more interesting and distinctive wine. As ever, though, it's all down to the producer.

A guide to native grapes : Dimiat A native, rather dull bulk white variety. **Gamza** (in Hungary, Kadarka) Makes light, soft cherry-fruit reds for drinking young.

Mavrud Unusual native red grape, capable of making big-shouldered, serious wines, dense and purple. **Melnik** The Syrah of Bulgaria, but heavier and chunkier. **Misket** Floral, perfumey white variety, no relation to Muscat. **Muscat Ottonel** Reasonable, but can age and decline too quickly in bottle. **Pamid** For Pamid, read pallid; light red variety, used for bulking out quality reds. Other grapes, occasionally seen: **Rhine Riesling** Good ones are fairly simple but have fruit and citric character. **Aligoté** Used for fizz and for dull dry whites. Better when blended with other grapes, like Chardonnay or native variety Rikat.

Chardonnay There are still too many thin and acidic wines, and lots of the New Wave ones are blandly tropical and tart. Preslav is the star Chardonnay region. This wine ($6) has unusually good texture for a Bulgarian white, and an appealing melon and lemon character. Schumen's cheap and cheerful Chardonnay Sauvignon blend is $5.50.

🍷 Schumen Chardonnay Sauvignon Blanc
🍷🍷 Preslav Barrel-Fermented Chardonnay

Cabernet Sauvignon Wines still tend to be baked, over-ripe and soupy, or earthy and

> "Few achieve the richly plummy, chocolate-and-smoke heightsof yesteryear, although Cabernet Sauvignon is still the safest bet of all the Bulgarian wines on offer."

rustic, with prune and beetroot character. Few achieve the richly plummy, chocolate-and-smoke heights of yesteryear, although Cabernet Sauvignon is still the safest bet of all the Bulgarian wines on offer. Blue Ridge ($6) is a new label from Domaine Boyar. The Nazdrave wine ($6.25) is dry and blackcurranty. Svischtov's Cabernet pink ($5.50) is fruity but crisp and light.

🍷 Svischtov Valley of the Roses Rosé • Blue Ridge Bin 316 Cabernet Sauvignon • Domaine Boyar Premium Cabernet Sauvignon • Nazdrave Cabernet Sauvignon

ENGLAND

The official industry line is that English wine is now as good as any the world over. Were this true, their only problem would be the almost total lack of interest shown by English wine drinkers.

Unfortunately there appear to be fewer good English wines about than there were a few years ago, when things looked promising for a time. A series of appalling summers hasn't helped. Like northern France, southern England must battle the elements, except England's weather is even worse than France's. And the Brits have to ask themselves—is the Champagne region best known for its thin acidic white table wine? Quite. Smart producers are turning to fizz production, and things are looking pretty optimistic there (*see* FIZZ). Very sadly, there are no table wines presently available in the high street of a standard to recommend here. The best bet for the curious is to tour the vineyards themselves, many of which are very beautiful and have good visitor facilities, and taste the wines in situ.

The best hope for the future of English wine must be a period of wanton destruction. Duff grapes misguidedly planted for our German-like climate, which are responsible for so much dreadfully duff wine, must be ripped up and replaced with French ones. Cheeringly, this has already started. Chardonnay, Pinot Noir and Sauvignon Blanc from across the Channel are being put in, along with Alsace varieties like Riesling and Pinot Blanc. Barrel fermentation is also coming into vogue, as it is in the Loire, where they have found it can counter high acidity levels in their fruit. Judicious oak aging of barrel-made wines might result in something with more texture and depth than is usual in English efforts.

P.S. Avoid anything labeled British Wine. This is sweetened up grape must imported in tanks from elsewhere. Like British Sherry. Only worse.

GRAPE VARIETIES

Bacchus Elderflowery, tartly fruity white grape, bred by crossing Sylvaner, Riesling and Müller-Thurgau.

Huxelrebe Dry, bitter, pithy. Usually better in blends.

Madeleine Angevine Plump, fruity, perhaps slightly honeyed, or else crisp, flinty, mildly appley whites.

Müller-Thurgau Dull bland workhorse German white grape variety. (Rip 'em up!)

Ortega Can be intensely peachy, floral, fresh, slightly green. Usually blended.

Pinot Noir Mostly used for fizz. Also for pinks.

Seyval Blanc Good ones start out green and lean, acquiring richer honeyed flavors in maturity.

GREECE

Formerly best known for its flabby, old-fashioned, resinous and pine-scented whites (and flabby, old-fashioned, resinous and earthy reds), Greece is now being hailed as one of the great hopes of the New Wave. Certainly quality is on the up and if prices are still surprisingly high ($12 is commonly asked, $18 or more for the best estate stuff) there are also lots more good drinkable bottles at $8 and $9. Even from Crete—the good stuff is evidently all made for export, which explains why it's impossible to find nice wine on vacation.

What all these New Wave Greeks share is quirkiness and individuality. They all have their own personality and charm. There is nothing that equates to Chardonnay or Cabernet Sauvignon. Choose Greek wine for its unusual flavors: these are wines for experimenting with. Many of them are good with food, but it's necessary to taste them before matching them. That's the only downside with quirkiness. Go with producer names rather than regions or grape varieties. New Wave activity is still a minority activity and there's still lots of tired, resiny wine about. The E.U. is pouring in the cash, so there is lots of cause for optimism here.

Greek Whites Producers are learning from New World consultants, and are beginning to pick white grapes earlier to stop the fruit dulling or over-ripening. The Antonopoulos wine ($10.50) is unoaked, big and tropical in style. Lots of good stuff is coming from the Peloponnese, and the island of Santorini. The Asprolithi wine is pear-fruited, very crisp, subtly spritzy and would be enjoyed by Italian wine fans. It beats Frascati into a cocked hat.

🍷 Xerolithia White, Crete • Asprolithi White, Patras • Santorini Dry White

🍷🍷 Domaine Gerovassiliou Epanomi • Antonopoulos Unoaked Chardonnay, Peloponnese • Ktima Constantine Lazaridi Amethystos • Tsantali Chromitsa • Sigalas Varelli, Santorini

Greek Reds Nemea/Pelopponese is becoming a quality red zone. Its Aghiorghitiko grape makes beautifully structured complex reds that taste anything but ethnic. Often the grape is blended, sometimes with Cabernet and Merlot for more structure (and familiarity). Look out too for Xynomavro wines from Naoussa in the north. Ktima Kyr-Yianni is a particularly exciting winery. The Syrah ($12) is a staggering wine. One to tease your friends with—they'll never guess!

🍷 Mirambelo Red, Crete
🍷🍷 Gaia Notios • Spiropoulos Porfyros, Peloponnese • Ktima Kyr-Yianni Ramnista, Naoussa • Tsantali Metoxi, Mt. Athos • Ktima Kyr-Yianni Syrah • Ktima Constantine Lazaridi Amethystos
🍷🍷🍷 Gaia Estate Aghiorghitiko, Nemea

HUNGARY

A few years ago Hungary was singled out for greatness. That hasn't happened, but there are still plenty of good budget wines, particularly whites, available. It's disappointing that more top estates aren't represented here. Nonetheless Hungary is the undoubted star of the Eastern European camp (which admittedly isn't saying much).

Grape varieties are getting more international. There's masses of Chardonnay, Sauvignon and Gewürztraminer, Cabernet Sauvignon and Merlot, as the native grape varieties seem to dwindle away. It's down to demand—at this price point consumers overseas are looking for wines they know and are unlikely to want to risk their six dollars on a red called Kekfrankos. The wines tend to be fairly bland and anonymous—competent and international, rather than sensational. But having said that, at $6 competence is very welcome.

"Hungary is the undoubted star of the Eastern European camp…"

Hungarians prefer a much more robust, flavorsome wine style than their export bottles suggest. Traditionally their whites aren't crisp and fruity and clean, but rich, yellowing, sweet, yeasty, firmly tannic and spicy, for drinking with rich spicy foods. Over half of Hungary's vineyards are on the Great Plain between the Danube and the Tisza, on sandy soils not much use for anything else. Masses of Kadarka and sweet plump whites are grown here for domestic consumption. The quality wine is grown in the hill vineyards. Good names to look out for include Hungarian winemaker Akos Kamocsay (Neszmely, Hilltop Winery) and flying wine-maker Kym Milne.

Hungary's most famous wine must have a mention. Tokaji (or Tokay) was the first wine in history to be made from botrytised ("nobly rotted") grapes. It's usually 70% Furmint, about 25% Hárslevelü and the rest Muscat. Aszú, a paste of botrytised grapes, is added to a vat of wine, the amount measured in Putts, or Puttonyos (literally buckets). Szamorodni Tokay wines aren't made with Aszú and are drier altogether.

GRAPE VARIETIES

WHITES

Chardonnay The better ones have restrained but ripe fruit and a characteristic citric edge. The barrel-fermented wines are more to Hungarian taste, enthusiastically yeasty and oaked. Most of the cheap stuff is increasingly crisp and bland. Hilltop Chardonnay is a bit of a star.

🍷 Chapel Hill Oaked Chardonnay • Hilltop Chardonnay

Furmint Native Hungarian Tokay staple. Flavorsome, rich and rounded grape with robust acids. Potentially a good Chardonnay partner.

Gewürztraminer Too often reined back into something modern and clean.
🍷 Deer Leap Gewürztraminer

Hárslevelü A Tokaji ingredient, along with Furmint, but softer and more aromatic.

Irsai Oliver A Muscat cross. Not usually very inspiring. This sub $5.50 wine is grapey but also dry.
🍷 Chapel Hill Irsai Oliver

Misket Supposedly not a Muscat relation; tastes like (an inferior) one.

Muscat Ottonel Usually dull and blowsy.

Pinot Blanc Should be rich and ripe, floral and appley, scented, fat and fresh. More often dull and neutral.

Pinot Grigio (Pinot Gris) Should be ripe and spicy. Good in blends with Chardonnay or native Zenit.
🍷 Nagyrede Pinot Grigio Zenit • Riverview Chardonnay Pinot Grigio

Sauvignon Blanc Hungarian Sauvignon tends to be crisp and overly subtle, but it has moments of brilliance. The Virgin Vintage wine ($9) is fresh, subtly tropical and citric.

🍷 Matra Sauvignon Blanc • Deer Leap Sauvignon Blanc • Riverview Sauvignon Blanc, Sopron, Hilltop winery

🍷🍷 Virgin Vintage Sauvignon Blanc, Hilltop winery

White Blends Cheap and cheerful, with delicate fruit and a charmingly eastern off-dry style. Both these wines are under $5.50.

🍷 Matra Springs Hungarian White • Deer Leap Dry White

REDS

Cabernet Franc Capable of making good young reds.

Cabernet Sauvignon A fairly recent addition to Hungary's vineyards, it tends to be on the light side and lack depth of fruit. This rich and fruity Kym Milne wine is $8.

🍷 Chapel Hill Oak Aged Cabernet Sauvignon

Kadarka Once noble Hungarian red variety, now in decline.

Kékfrankos The same grape as Austria's Blaufränkisch. Can be thin and vegetal.

Merlot Can be good but too often either jammy or dry.

Pinot Noir Also known as Nagyburgundi. Red Hungarian Pinot Noir is rarely worth drinking.

Red Blends This wine by Akos Kamocsay is easy, grapey drinking ($5.50).
🍷 Butlers Blend, Hilltop winery

MEXICO

Generally it's far too hot and arid here for viticulture, but cool-climate zones are under development. LA Cetto's wine is the

only good Mexican available at present. It's a remarkable wine for $8, being dark, port-wine sweet and brambly, its rich fruit balanced by firm tannins.
🍷 L A Cetto Petite Syrah

ROMANIA

Problems with quality keep sticking pins in Romania's balloon. Bad wines are worse than bad Bulgarians, but the handful of good ones are good value for money. Quality seems to be improving again at the cheap end, after a few lousy years. Better viticultural practices, and New World ideas about how to extract maximum fruit and color are having an impact at last. Well, that's what this press release says. In reality, most Romanian bottles are still a big disappointment. Perhaps they should focus on the $9 bottle and the quality, hand-made, low-yield product, instead of pushing out more and more sub-$6 bulk wine.

🍷 Romanian Prairie Merlot, Dealu Mare • Young Vatted Cabernet Sauvignon, Pietroasa • River Route Limited Edition Chardonnay

TUNISIA

Tunisia is a Muslim country, and no wine is made. Seems like a conundrum until you discover that though the fruit is from Tunisia, it is despatched in refrigerated ships to Sicily, and

there transformed into rich and delicious wine. Both these wines are 100% Carignan. The Accademia del Sole wine is organic. Brian Fletcher, an enterprising Australian, is behind this inspired venture.

🍷🍷 Accademia del Sole • Selian Carignan, Calatrasi

URUGUAY

Tannat, a southwestern French varietal, was brought into Uruguay by Basque migrants, and is the principal red grape grown. The Uruguayan wine industry is still in its infancy but some of the wine reaching foreign shores is extremely impressive. Almost all the vineyards are on hillside sites in the cooler south of Uruguay, where the heat is further moderated by cooling Atlantic air. The Don Pascual Reserve Tannat ($10.50) is bold and rich; the Pisano Family wine ($13) is juicy and smoky. Bright Brothers are seeking cooler vineyard sites for their northern French varietals.

🍷 Bright Bros. Sauvignon Sémillon • Bright Bros. Tannat Cabernet Franc

🍷🍷 Don Pascual Reserve Tannat • Pisano Family Reserve Tannat

FIZZ

CHAMPAGNE

Champagne was, it is alleged, invented by the English. Certainly the winemakers across the Channel wouldn't have been able to stop their bottles exploding if it hadn't been for good English glass. Whatever the exact chronology of events, it is known for sure that Champagne evolved out of the practice of sweetening the harshly green and acidic white wines made in a region where the cool wet climate made it notoriously difficult to ripen grapes properly. This is the most northerly AC, some 90 miles to the northeast of Paris. It's part of the Champagne-making tradition that a *dosage* of sugar and yeast is added to the basic wine before corking and allowing a second fermentation. The trapped carbon dioxide that results remains dissolved in the wine until the pop of the cork releases it. The best Champagne has the tiniest, tingliest stream of bubbles, known as a "mousse." The sediment is maneuvered (traditionally by hand, but now more usually by machines) into the neck of the bottle, where it is frozen into a small block and then removed before re-corking.

Most standard Non Vintage Champagne is made using Chardonnay, Pinot Noir and perhaps also Pinot Meunier grapes. Blanc de Blancs wines are Chardonnay only. Blanc de Noirs wines are red grape only wines.

Champagne is the only region in the world allowed to use the C word, which is restricted by law to approved wines made within the Champagne AC. All other wines, whether made in France or overseas must be labeled Traditional Method, or Méthode Traditionelle. They are not allowed to use the word Champagne even if their wine is made identically to those of Rheims and Épernay. Sparkling Wines are generally tank-fermented and not bottle-fermented, unless the wine is labeled Traditional Method.

Champagne producers went through a brief period of panic as New World fizz-makers showed they had mastered the Traditional Method and began to turn out wonderful wine at low prices. But then, very sensibly, they realized that what they have is unique, and that part of its mystique is the high price that must be paid for the real thing.

Rosé Champagnes are traditionally made by macerating some of the Pinot Noir grape skins to take a little of their color. Unfortunately, many modern producers simply add a little red wine instead. This explains why lots of pink Champagnes don't taste as good or as different as they should, and why some are just too "winey."

Dryness indicators: *Sec* should mean dry, but in this case it's only medium dry. Extra Dry is drier than *Sec*, but not as dry as *Brut*. *Demi-Sec* means pretty sweet (most *Demi-Secs* are also pretty dire). *Doux* is the label for out and out sweeties. *Rich Doux* wines are the sweetest of all.

BOB (Buyers' Own Brand) means that the contents have been blended to the client's wishes. Supermarket own brands, for example. Cuvée de Prestige, or Cuvée de Luxe, or just plain De Luxe suggest the contents should be something special. Some are, but not all. The best, like Veuve Clicquot La Grande Dame or Roederer Cristal, or indeed Krug Grande Cuvée—it's only money after all—need plenty of bottle age. Ten years minimum. Recently disgorged: the wines have been cellar-aged for much longer than is normal (maybe even 25–30 years). The best, like Bollinger RD, acquire tremendous complexity.

Non Vintage can be a great buy. The best use some back-stock (aged wine kept in reserve) to add depth and finesse and maintain a consistent house style, whatever the current vintage's quality. Most NV Champagne is aged for three years before release. Vintage wines come from a single year, judged to be an outstanding one. Judged by the makers, at least. Keep your NV wines for even 9 months and they should improve in bottle.

There are 17 Grand Cru villages in Champagne, and 38 Premier Cru. There are no further classifications than these. Grande Marque—the collective name for the 24 Champagne houses that consider themselves above the common herd—may or may not be a promise of quality.

VINTAGES

2000 suffered from a stormy harvest but quality
will be pretty good. 1999 was a big crop and quality is good. 1998 looks promising. 1997 is very
patchy. 1995 and '96 were excellent, ripe years and
should be snapped up. 1994 was poor in the main.
1991–3 weren't great either. 1988 and '89 were
exceptional years and '90 was a classic vintage.

GRAPE VARIETIES

Chardonnay Can be steely and hard when young, in
an immature Blanc de Blancs, but matures wonderfully well. Most Champagnes are made by blending
Chardonnay with Pinot Noir. Blanc de Blancs wines,
made only from Chardonnay, might be stern at first,
but they can age superbly into wines that yield nuts
and honey and subtlety. These light fresh Champagnes
are very much in fashion.

Pinot Meunier Champagne's second black grape lends
easy, plump softness and aroma. Considered an inferior, padding-out grape by the top brands, who rarely
use it. Appears in a supporting role in many standard
Non Vintage wines, and in some Blanc de Noirs.

Pinot Noir The world's trickiest red grape is difficult
to ripen in Champagne but its weight and power filter
through. The fruit is very gingerly crushed to keep the

color pale and interesting. Blanc de Noirs can take a decade to mature. They can be rather lumpen and sturdy, almost New World like in their simplicity, though there are classics, notably Vieilles Vignes from Bollinger.

TWELVE GOOD HOUSES FOR NON-VINTAGE CHAMPAGNE

The delicious Champagne Fleury ($27) would make it a baker's dozen if it weren't for the fact that it's only available as a limited parcel.

Billecart-Salmon Crisp, tangy and fairly lean Chardonnay-dominated Champagnes ($32).

Blin H Blin & Co is a modern co-op in the Marne Valley. Good stuff, with flowery Pinot Meunier fruit and dryness ($24).

Bollinger Generously rich and biscuity, delicately fruity, nicely oaked NV (Special Cuvée) contains a

high proportion of reserve wine and is 60% Pinot
Noir. The fullest-flavored of the high street popular
brands ($42).

Bonnet F Bonnet Non Vintage is a good budget buy,
being soft and easy, plump and dry. Lots of the supermarket own-brand wine comes from F Bonnet ($24).

Gimmonet Pierre Gimmonet et Fils is lively, elegant,
with a pronounced Chardonnay character. Exceptional
value. Tastes almost New World ($22–$26).

Heidsieck Forward-thinking producer Daniel Thibault
now lists the year of laying-down in the cellar on even
the Non Vintage wines. 1995 and 1996 wines are
superb ($38).

Lanson Lanson Black Label is one of the best all-
purpose Champagnes, nutty and ripe, biscuity and
citric ($33).

Laurent-Perrier Apple-nosed, crisp and tasty, light and easy drinking ($38). The delicious Rosé is a proper one (proper pinks are now rare) made with skins from Pinot Noir fruit ($48).

Piper Heidsieck Pear, apple and grapefruit flavors with a nutty toasty quality. Very good value for the style ($30).

Roederer Fruity, biscuity, yeasty, nutty and rich Pinot Noir-dominated wines and good Blanc de Blancs ($38).

Taittinger Clean, modern, fresh, brioche-bready, subtly appley, Chardonnay-dominated, but also has Pinot Noir for balance ($38).

Veuve Clicquot The excellent Yellow Label NV has lovely texture and roundness, apple and pear fruit and a lively tingly mousse. Grown up and moreish ($38).

FIZZ FROM AROUND THE WORLD

Australia Good Australian fizz is world class. Champagne method is used in the more expensive bottles. Australian producers are now learning that their sparkling wine is best from cool-climate sites: crisp, elegant wines are replacing the yeasty, full-flavored overbearing style of just a few years ago. Almost all the supermarket

"Good Australian fizz is world class."

own brand Oz sparklers at the $8–$9 level are tank-fermented wines from Oz giant Seppelt. They are competent, crisp and neutral. Great Western Brut Seppelt's own recipe fizz is lively, toasty and crisp ($9). Green Point 49% Chardonnay, 50% Pinot Noir, 1% Pinot Meunier. Generously flavored bready, rounded fizz made by Moët & Chandon's Australian winery ($18). Jansz From Tasmania: Only about a third of the fruit is Tasmanian, the rest is imported. Clean, dry, crisp with lemon and biscuit flavors and a pleasing fullness. Made by Louis Roederer in partnership with a local producer ($15). Rosemount Vintage Sparkling Chardonnay: Budget, clean sparkler, with a plump fresh character. Apple and pear fruit, creamy yet dry, with good acidity ($10.50). Seaview Blanc de Blancs: Creamy but tangy, fruity but dry, Seaview's 100% Chardonnay fizz is pretty much unbeatable at this price level. Snap up the 1995 wine if you can still find it ($13). They also make a decent Non Vintage ($10.50). Yellowglen: Soft textured but crisp, fruity but bready and yeasty ($12.50)

England England is capable of making good, tasty, well-balanced wine, just not very much of it so far. Most is only available direct from vineyards, or on a regional basis. Carr Taylor of East Sussex beat off 4000 competitors to take the top fizz prize at Vinexpo 2000 with their $21 wine. Ridgeview Estate, also in Sussex, makes good sparklers—look out for their prize-winning Cuvée Merret Belgravia. Nyetimber (Sussex again) make excellent fizz if you can find it.

France Several of the French regions also make non-Champagne fizz, though most of it is far inferior to the New World for fruit and finesse. Clairette de Die can be a fun wine if you like the grapey, sherbety Asti Spumante style. Crémant de Bourgogne from Burgundy ought to be good (with all that Pinot Noir and Chardonnay going spare) but usually disappoints: try the Cave de Lugny wine. Some decent stuff is beginning to come out of the Loire—look out for Langlois Crémant de Loire Rosé ($12). Blanquette de Limoux (and Crémant de Limoux) wines, also from the Languedoc, used to be yeasty and a bit tired tasting but are now improving very fast. Delicious wines, typically blending the local white varieties with the fruit from newly established Chardonnay and Chenin Blanc, are coming through now at the $9–$12 level.

Italy Italian fizz used to mean a stark choice between bone dry, bitter Prosecco and sweet, pappy Asti Spumante, but these days Prosecco has more fruit and ease, and Spumante is crisper and less sweet. Prosecco, made by hillside wineries around Treviso in the Veneto, is still a very dry wine but there is less bitterness and more of an international feel to these wines. Look out for Metodo Classico. Good modern Asti is drier than it used to be. Many have a delicious pear and elderflower character; they make great pick-me-ups on a gray day. Moscato d'Asti wines are sweeter and have a grapey flavor. All these wines have price on their side—good stuff is widely available at $6–$9.

New Zealand Most New Zealand fizz is made Traditional Method, in the Marlborough area, using Pinot Noir and Chardonnay fruit. There are two basic styles, one clean and dry, the other yeastier and fuller flavored. Lindauer and Deutz lead the pack. The other widely seen wine, Pelorus, is good and mature thanks to three years lees-aging; pity about the Cloudy Bay price tag ($24). Hunter's Miru Miru ($18) is good if you can find it. Deutz: Champagne-like, Chardonnay-based, elegant, crisp and yet biscuity with a subtle yeast character and plenty of depth ($18). Lindauer Brut: Non Vintage owned by Montana. Fruity, toasty and yeasty ($18). Lindauer Special Reserve: Non Vintage softer, with riper fruit, but also crisper and more elegant, with less Pinot Noir in the mix than the "ordinary." Another convincingly Champagne-like wine ($13).

Spain Earthy, eggy, sulphury Cava with big coarse bubbles is a hard wine to forget and an easy one to avoid

now the New World is awash with good clean wine at $8–$9. It's all change in Cava-land though. There are still bad wines about, but far fewer than even two years ago. The new model is lemony, light, dry; in fact some are too lean and modern. The best New Wave Cavas have faint, clean traces of the old characteristic savory oak-yeasty style, and more cashew nut body and individuality about them. Segura Viudas Cava Brut Reserva: Soft, appley and neutral ($12). Segura Viudas Cava Non Vintage: The best Cava available. Full-flavored, rich and nutty, but also clean and refreshing ($10).

USA Decent American fizz is made in the Napa Valley and in cool climate districts like Anderson and Carneros, though there are signs that American producers are turning away from sparkling wine production and back to table wine. (It's too difficult, it's not profitable enough, there's not enough of a market). Mumm were the first among the Champagne houses to start up operations in the New World, in California 20 years ago. Their Cuvee Napa ($16.50) is one of the best New World wines you can get: intriguingly, it uses a little Pinot Gris in the mix for a distinctive, subtly spicy edge. Mumm's California wine is frequently better than their French Champagne. Look out too for Chandon wines, from Moët & Chandon. Chandon have also started a winery in Argentina and are making $12 fizz there which is also worth a try.

GLOSSARY

Acids Essential components in all wines. The "fixed" acids, such as tartaric, malic and citric, come largely from the grape. Malic acid is transformed into the softer lactic acid during the malolactic fermentation that occurs in many wines after the alcoholic fermentation. These acids give a wine crispness and bite and can aid cellaring potential.

Aging all wine is "aged" to some extent, although the duration can vary from a few days in bottle, e.g., Beaujolais Nouveau, to decades in oak casks, e.g., Tawny Port. Aging in oak barrels results in controlled oxidation of the wine. If the barrels are relatively new, the aging process can also impart flavors and tannins to wine, improving its potential to age further in bottle.

Bottle aging is a more complicated process. In the case of a red wine, the simple tannin molecules of a young, purple red join together to form progressively longer chains, and the color changes through shades of red and orange, eventually to brown. At the same time the flavors soften and meld to produce a harmonious taste. The tannins and coloring matter eventually precipitate in the form of sediment. After reaching its peak a wine will go into irreversible decline with further aging.

It is impossible to generalize about the correct length of time to age a wine. Full-bodied reds that are often found to improve with bottle age include the top wines of Bordeaux, Burgundy, Barolo, Brunello di Montalcino, New World Cabernets and Vintage Ports. The best Champagnes often benefit from a year of two in bottle, and Sauternes and sweet whites from the Loire can also benefit from prolonged aging.

Alcohol content Amount of alcohol present in a wine, usually expressed as a percentage by volume. "12% Vol" means that 12% of the volume of the wine is pure alcohol. A glass of Port, at 20% alcohol by volume, will have twice the intoxicating effect of the same sized glass of table wine at 10%. For comparison, the most common spirits are 40% or 43%.

Appellation part of a French system (*Appellation contrôlée*) that guarantees the origin of a wine from a demarcated area; its specific purpose is to guarantee authenticity. In general, the laws of any AC control the following: the area entitled to the name; grape varieties; density of vine plants; minimum alcohol levels; yields. The wine must be analyzed and tested before the AC is granted.

Barrel Cylindrical container, usually made of wood, used to store and mature wine. Traditionally barrels were made from several different types of wood, but today most are made of oak. A new barrel imparts tannin and a vanilla flavor to wine, and the smaller the barrel, the more marked is this effect. An old barrel, if it is clean, will impart no flavor but it will allow a slow, controlled oxidation of the wine.

Botrytis Fungus responsible for the creation of noble rot on grapes. This allows water to evaporate from the grape juice, leading to an increased concentration of sugar. The presence of this beneficial rot is the key to the production of the great sweet wines of Sauternes, Monbazillac and Anjou-Saumur in France, the Beerenauslese and Trokenbeerenauslese wine of Germany and Austria, Tokaji in Hungary and some New World sweet wines.

Bottle age Term attributed to wine that has spent some months or years in bottle, and the associated mature bouquet and flavor that it develops.

Bottle fermented Term used to describe sparkling wine in which the secondary fermentation has taken place in bottle (e.g., Champagne).

Corked Tasting term used to describe that a wine is "off," with a stale, woody, moldy smell and taste, possibly accompanied by oxidation.

Estate bottled Term used to indicate that a wine has been bottled on the estate where the grapes were grown. It is intended as a guarantee of authenticity.

Fermentation Process whereby grape sugar is converted into alcohol and carbon dioxide by the action of enzymes produced by yeast. For dry wines, the process is allowed to continue until all the sugar has been turned into alcohol. If the initial level of grape sugar is very high, fermentation may stop naturally before all the sugar has been converted, and a sweet wine is the result.

Fortified wine Wine to which brandy, or neutral grape spirit, has been added. In the case of Port, spirit is added to stop fermentation prematurely, before all the grape sugar has been turned into alcohol. In the case of Sherry, the wine is fortified after fermentation.

Flying winemaker Flying winemakers are well-named people in the wine-producing world. They pop up all over the planet, acting as consultants to wineries keen to revamp their methods and maximize their fruit. They are mainly responsible for the New Wave.

Late harvest Term equivalent to *Spätlese* or *vendage tardive*, found mainly on New World wine labels. It indicates that the grapes were harvested later than usual, and should therefore have a higher concentration of sugar. Such wines are usually rich and sweet, but they may be fermented to dryness, becoming powerful and alcoholic.

Lees Deposit of dead yeast that falls to the bottom of a vat of wine after fermentation and aging. Normally the wine is then bottled, leaving this sediment behind. Some wines, notably Muscadet, are sometimes aged for a time on the lees (Sur Lie), leading to a distinctive yeasty aroma and taste.

Maceration Process whereby red wines derive their color, tannin and some flavor through contact of the fermenting must with grape skins. A shorter period of maceration, or skin contact, can also be beneficial for white varieties.

Malolactic fermentation Fermentation which occurs after the alcoholic fermentation, when malic acid is transformed into the softer lactic acid. These acids give a wine crispness and bite and can aid cellaring potential.

Méthode traditionnelle Method by which Champagne gets its bubbles, by a second fermentation that takes place in bottle.

Must Mixture of unfermented grape juice, skins and pips.

Must weight Natural sugar content of grape juice

before fermentation begins. The sugar level is an important factor in deciding when to harvest grapes. It can be measured using a refractometer or a hydrometer. The potential alcohol content of a wine is determined by the must weight.

Noble rot *see* **Botrytis**

Non vintage (NV) Term used to describe a wine for which no year of harvest is specified. Basic European table wine and branded wines are NV, so that the blender is able to produce a consistent product by blending wines of different vintages.

Nose Tasting term which covers all the smell characteristics of a wine, including the aroma and bouquet.

Oak Family of trees whose wood is generally agreed to be the best material for the construction of barrels for the storage and aging of fine wines. When a high-quality young wine, with a good concentration of fruit, spends some months or years in oak barrels, this treatment can add extra dimension of flavor to the wine, rather like the use of seasoning in cooking. The fruit flavors are complemented by the vanilla flavor derived from the oak, and the wood can also give extra tannin to the wine, which may increase its aging potential.

Oak and barrel-making are both very expensive, and aging in oak barrels adds significantly to the

cost of producing a wine. Some winemakers therefore use the cheaper method of fermenting or aging
wine in the presence of oak chips.

Organic Wines made without the use of herbicides,
chemical fertilizers, or any additives in the winery.
However, there are many exceptions allowed by the
various bodies controlling organic viticulture and
wine-making. For instance, almost all organic wine
is made with the use of the chemical sulphur dioxide.

Palate Tasting term used to describe the flavor and
sensation of the wine in the mouth (as opposed to
the nose and appearance).

Residual sugar Sugar left in a wine once it has been
fermented and is ready for bottling. The quantity of
sugar is usually measured in grams per liter. This
level determines whether the wine can be described
as dry, medium-dry and so on.

Sugar Vital ingredient in grapes, sugar is converted
into alcohol by the action of yeast during fermentation. In areas where grapes do not always have a suf-
ficient level of natural sugar, the addition of sugar is
permitted to boost the final alcohol content. The
amount of sugar that can be added is controlled by
law.

Sulphur dioxide Essential additive to nearly all wines,

even those described as organic, although all good winemakers will keep its use to a minimum. It combines anti-oxidant and disinfectant properties and is used to kill wild yeast on grape skins before they are fermented, to sterilize barrels and bottles, and to eliminate any bacterial infection—and prevent oxidation—in fermented wine. In some countries, notably the U.S. and Australia, the use of sulphur dioxide must be declared on the label.

Sur lie *see* **Lees**

Tannin Usually identified as a dry sensation on the gums and roof of the mouth, sometimes accompanied by a leathery, or cold tea, smell or taste. In high quality young red wines, the high tannin content can mask the fruit flavors; as the wine matures, the tannin should integrate with the fruit and acidity to yield a harmonious, well-knit flavor. Tannin is found in grape skins, along with the pigments that give red wine its color.

Terroir French term used to embrace all the characteristics of a vineyard site (including soil type, climate, etc.).

Varietal Wine made entirely (or almost entirely) from a single grape variety.

Vat General term used to describe a vessel in which wine is stored, or undergoes fermentation. They may be made of cement, wood, fiberglass or stainless steel.

Vintage In general, the year in which the grapes used to make a wine were harvested. In most wine-producing regions, climatic conditions can vary considerably from one year to the next, leading to good and bad vintages.

Yeast Group of bacteria responsible for the enzymes which promote fermentation of grape juice, the conversion of grape sugars into alcohol. Wild yeasts occur naturally on the outside of grape skins, and these will start fermentation soon after the grapes are crushed. Some winemakers prefer to get rid of the natural yeasts using sulphur dioxide, and then start the fermentation with cultured yeasts produced in a laboratory. This leads, they believe, to a cleaner fermentation with better expression of varietal character.

Yield Measure of how much wine is produced in a vineyard. Low yield is commonly equated with high quality.